COLORADO'S
OTHER MOUNTAINS

COLORADO'S OTHER MOUNTAINS

A Climbing Guide to Selected Peaks Under 14,000 Feet

By
Walter R. Borneman

CORDILLERA PRESS, INC.
Publishers in the Rockies

First Edition
  2 3 4 5 6 7 8 9

Library of Congress Cataloging in Publication Data

Borneman, Walter R., 1952-
    Colorado's other mountains.

    Includes index.
    1. Mountaineering—Colorado—Guide-books. 2. Colorado
    —Description and travel—1981- . Guide-books.
I. Title.
GV199.42.C6B673 1984   796.5'22'09788   84-7623

ISBN: 0-917895-00-2

All photos by the author unless otherwise noted.

Printed in the United States of America

Contents

Part 3:
The Western Slope 125

7-7-2001

Acknowledgements

We should always savor new summits by remembering that we have not vanquished an enemy, but enjoyed a fleeting moment with a newfound friend. Those moments with new mountains are richer and more meaningful when they are shared with old and valued friends.

This book would not have been possible without the support and friendship of Gary and Dolora Koontz. Gary and Dolora were my companions on almost all of these peaks, my critics as to route selections and descriptions, contributors of fine photographs, and always my friends.

Gary, Dolora, and I value the friendship of those who joined us on some of our climbs. First and foremost were Tim and Melissa Duffy. Tim and Melissa took time out from winning races to climb with us on such great ones as Ice Mountain and Mount Adams. Vic Rosengren and Mike Joyer scrambled up a few of them with us, as did Craig and Debbie Koontz, Omar and Anne Richardson, and, of course, Skipper. Even Lyn Lampert, my elusive co-author from the *Fourteeners*, sat with me atop Mount Owen before his early retirement from climbing!

Summit ridge,
Cathedral Peak.

For

Naomi and Nathaniel Richardson,
Jennifer, Brad, and Chris Pierce, and
Hillary Anne Koontz

With the hope that they too will come to know and
champion the grandeur of lofty mountains, the freedom
of wild rivers, and the quiet dignity of the land

About the Author

Walter R. Borneman is a Colorado attorney and historian. He is the co-author, with Lyndon J. Lampert, of *A Climbing Guide to Colorado's Fourteeners*, the history and climbing routes of the state's fourteen-thousand-foot peaks, and the author of *Marshall Pass, Denver and Rio Grande Gateway to the Gunnison Country*, the history of Colorado's first transcontinental rail crossing.

Base Camp:
A Few Words of Introduction

Colorado's Other Mountains is a guide to the history and climbing routes of thirty-two of Colorado's great mountains. The title emphasizes the premise that Colorado has many peaks equal to or even more challenging and interesting than the state's fabled Fourteeners. Indeed, one of the great joys of writing this book was that there was no "list" to be completed and no summit which *had* to be reached.

The criteria for inclusion here was to look to Colorado's varied and numerous summits and pick ones which sparked a particular interest—an intriguing history, an inviting challenge, a panoramic view, or a close proximity to home when brain and body cried out for escape. Included are obvious "greats" such as Mount Powell and Ice Mountain, and less obvious pleasures such as Mount Hope, Buffalo Peaks, and Mount Adams. One early thought—to include only Thirteeners—was discarded for fear of repeating the Fourteener craze (for which I accept my share of the blame!) and making a serious affront to such deserving summits as Mount Richthofen and Mount Zirkel.

If there is one characteristic of uniformity in the list, it is that all mountains must be approached with care and confidence. *This guide is not a substitute for mountaineering knowledge and experience.* Readers are urged to recognize the limits of their individual abilities, the uncertainty of Colorado's fickle weather, and the vagaries of seasonal conditions in planning

1

and executing climbs. For those who desire to increase their abilities or seek climbing companions, a variety of instruction and companionship is available from the Colorado Mountain Club and other organizations.

This guide does not recount the general history and geology of the ranges or the history and climbing routes of the Fourteeners. For both, *A Climbing Guide to Colorado's Fourteeners* is unabashedly recommended. As always, one cannot go wrong with Bob Ormes' *Guide to Colorado Mountains*, particularly as a "possibles" bag for new climbs. Also, I continue to exude great enthusiasm for Bill Bueler's *Roof of the Rockies*, a thorough history of major climbing accomplishments in the state.

No book can adequately prepare a climber for the great variable of weather. It is of key importance to all but the most foolhardy, and it has played a major role in the production of this book. I climbed most of the peaks discussed below in 1982 and 1983. The fall of 1982 had the worst fall weather I had experienced in fifteen years of climbing, except for one October weekend that found me on Pacific Peak. Those of us who bemoaned the late arrival of summer in 1982 had no inkling that summer in the high country in 1983 would be even later! Fourth of July climbs in 1983 met with Memorial Day conditions, and at least one Memorial Day outing boasted of a first winter ascent! In retrospect, of course, such weather demands and uncertainties merely accentuated the challenge.

Finally, I could not offer a sampling of favorite places without urging upon you a heartfelt theme and concern. In the far too few and always too short years since I first climbed to the summit of what we thought was Mount Yale (it wasn't), the land of Colorado has shuddered under an onslaught of ever-increasing use. In selfish moments, I yearn for Colorado as it was sixty years ago when my friend Stephen H. Hart climbed with Albert Ellingwood up the Ellingwood Arete on Crestone Needle, or even as it was fifteen years ago when that bunch of high school kids with army surplus packs climbed "Mount Yale."

In more pragmatic moments, I recognize that change is historic and in fact inevitable. Our task and our responsibility, however, is to see that *this* change, this rapid and dramatic impact of population, exploitation, and use, does not irreversibly alter the basic nature of our land.

There are, to be sure, those of us who pack out our trash, leave our campsites as if we hadn't been there, avoid tramping through fragile areas, and respect the natural inhabitants; and there may even be those among us who pick up after others as well. Yet, the disgusting fact remains that we are outnumbered—outnumbered by a generation of users who have little regard for the basic nature of the land.

No one can turn back the clock or stop the change which grips Colorado today; yet everyone can make a conscious effort to walk in harmony with the land. Everyone can eliminate discarded trash, charred campfire remains, and reckless, senseless destruction. Certainly, it is not a final answer, nor will it solve the larger issues, but it is a beginning, and afterall, isn't that the real concern—that there always be beginnings and not a landless end?

Part 1
Front Range and Vicinity

From the craggy summits of the Indian Peaks to the traditional beginner Fourteener of Mount Sherman, the Front Range and its vicinity offer a wide diversity of challenge. In this book, the "vicinity" is loosely defined to include the North Park area, the fabulous Gore Range, and the historic Mosquito Peaks.

The mountains in this section were chosen largely for their proximity to the metropolitan Denver area and in many cases are recommended as beginner or family climbs. Parkview, Square Top, Audubon, and Byers are particularly good beginner climbs that offer outstanding views of the surrounding region. The difficult exceptions which come readily to mind are Mount Powell, the high point of the Gores; Pacific Peak, a sharp summit in the Tenmile Range; and Mount Zirkel, a landmark deep in the northern part of the state.

In addition to the peaks which follow, the potential for climbing in the Front Range and vicinity is vast. The mecca of Rocky Mountain National Park is not even mentioned here, save for Mount Richthofen. A number of fine summits besides Mount Powell offer excitement in the Gore Range, as do other summits in the Indian Peaks. Finally, the Tenmile Range presents some fine ridge-running possibilities.

To many, of course, the Front Range peaks are "the mountains" of Colorado. The close proximity of almost two million people makes the range and its environs especially susceptible to the pressures of growth. It is up to those of us in the two million, and to those visitors to our state, to see that our experiences and conduct in those mountains insures that they remain "the mountains" representative of Colorado's wilderness legacy.

Mount Audubon rises above the stillness of Brainard Lake. The trail ascends the sloping ridge to the right.

MOUNT AUDUBON
13,223 Feet
Indian Peaks—Front Range

Mount Audubon is a good beginner or family climb that offers superb views of the challenging Indian Peak summits. Its rounded top is easily recognizable from the plains north of Denver. For those who shun the crowds of summer weekends, Audubon becomes far more interesting as an early season or winter climb.

The mountain was named by Dr. Charles C. Parry in honor of John J. Audubon, the nineteenth-century naturalist and painter. Parry was an eminent botanist who started where

Edwin James (*see* James Peak) left off to collect and catalog the many varieties of Colorado plants. Parry initially studied botany under John Torrey, who had done work with James's collection, and this association fired Parry's interest in Colorado. Beginning in 1861, Parry made numerous trips to the Front Range, where he used barometers to make the first accurate measurements of a number of peaks. The summits he named included Grays, Torreys, Guyot, and Audubon. Unlike Parry's mentors Asa Gray, John Torrey, and Arnold Guyot, Parry gave the name to Audubon as a posthumous honor.

Parry appears to have made the first recorded ascent of Mount Audubon in company with the little-known J.W. Velie, on an 1862 or 1864 visit. The 1864 excursion included an attempt on Longs Peak with *Rocky Mountain News* editor William N. Byers.

Brainard Lake at the base of Mount Audubon has long been a favorite refuge for Front Range residents during summer's heat. With the cross-country skiing boom of the last decade, similar crowds converge on the area during the winter.

THE ROUTES
Roosevelt National Forest
Ward 7½ Quad

Brainard Lake: From just north of Ward on Colorado 72, drive west five miles on a paved and clearly marked road to Brainard Lake and then follow signs through several parking loops to the Mount Audubon trailhead. From the trailhead, follow the Mount Audubon/Buchanan Pass Trail north one and one-half miles to a junction. The route climbs moderately and switchbacks onto the broad east flank of Audubon through some delightful bristlecone pines. At the junction, take the west (left) fork and follow it two miles, first to the saddle north of the summit and then south up the remaining 600 feet of the summit cone. The route is easily marked and heavily travelled, but note this caveat. In bad weather or early in the season, Mount Audubon is no place for the inexperienced. Thunderstorms build up rapidly in the Indian Peaks region and demand special caution.

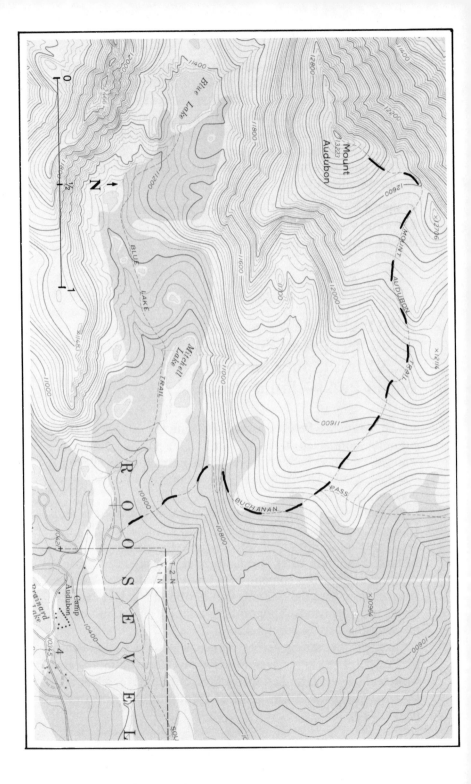

Experienced climbers wishing to avoid the summer weekend crowds will still find Audubon a rewarding mountain to climb because of the fine views of the Indian Peaks. Early season climbs or even ski approaches are quite plausible, and so are respectable glissades down the gentle slopes east of the summit saddle. All parties, particularly those descending in poor weather, should avoid the wall of cliffs on the cirque southeast of the summit.

Brainard Lake trailhead to summit: 3½ miles
Elevation gain: 2,800 feet
(Route description from July climb)

ARAPAHO PEAKS
13,502 feet (North Summit)
13,397 feet (South Summit)
Indian Peaks—Front Range

The Arapaho Peaks are visible from the plains as twin summits connected by a serrated ridge rising above the smooth, rounded hump formed by the east shoulder of South Arapaho Peak. The Arapaho Glacier snuggles into the cirque between the two peaks.

Those dear and delightful ladies, Louisa Ward Arps and Elinor Kingery, report in *High Country Names* that Case's 1862 map of Colorado Territory gave the peaks the name Mount Edmunds after a member of President Lincoln's Administration. But somehow, the name "Arapaho" became so associated with the summits that Ferdinand V. Hayden, the early surveyor and topographer, adopted it in his atlas, insuring the name's continuance.

With early climbing activity concentrated on Longs Peak, the Arapaho Peaks received little interest from mountaineers. Miners, however, combed the valleys to the east for silver and by 1870 the town of Caribou had sprung to life beneath the peaks.

South Arapaho Peak (left) and North Arapaho (right) rise above Arapaho Glacier and are connected via a serrated ridge.

While miners probably made the first ascent of both summits, Arnold and Herman Emch made what was probably the first ascent of the east face of North Arapaho from Arapaho Glacier as well as the first descent of the mountain's east ridge in September of 1900. Arnold Emch went on to climb most of the neighboring peaks between 1900 and 1915.

During that period, naturalist Enos Mills and others, including several prominent founders of the fledgling Colorado Mountain Club, were pushing the concept of Rocky Mountain National Park. Many of the peaks near the Arapahos bore no names and in an effort to fill the blank spots on maps, Ellsworth Bethel, a Denver high school botany teacher and Colorado Mountain Club activist, proposed,

South Arapaho's north face, viewed from North Arapaho, was still heavily corniced and snowpacked in mid-July, 1983.

"Who builds these things anyway?" Summit cairn, North Arapaho Peak.

perhaps with the Arapaho Peaks as an inspiration, to name the summits after Indian tribes important to Colorado's heritage. Thus, the Indian Peaks got their names and the Arapahos became surrounded by Navajo, Kiowa, Arikaree, Paiute, Niwot, and others. While the Indian Peaks section was not included in Rocky Mountain National Park when it was created in 1915, this land of craggy summits and lush valleys remains a wilderness area.

THE ROUTES
Arapaho National Forest
Monarch Lake 7½ Quad
Ward 7½ Quad

Rainbow Lakes: From the junction of Colorado 72 and 119 at Nederland, drive north on Colorado 72 for 7.2 miles to a road going west (left) to the University of Colorado Camp. A short distance from the highway, take the left-hand fork (the right fork goes to the camp) and continue over a boulder-strewn road, passable in cars with care, a total of 5.2 miles to the trailhead at the far west end of Rainbow Lakes Campground.

Follow the trail marked "Glacier Rim/Arapaho Pass" for six miles to the 12,700-foot saddle just east of South Arapaho Peak. This saddle can also be reached from the Fourth of July Campground northwest of Eldora with the same elevation gain, but two miles less distance—a fact which, when coupled with some good glissade possibilities on the latter route, required one climbing guide author to quell a small mutiny among his party after hiking from Rainbow Lakes.

From the saddle, the Arapaho Glacier is a grand sight to the north, while South Arapaho Peak looms a half-mile, 700-foot vertical climb to the west. A steep and rocky trail leads to its summit with no particular difficulties unless snow covers the route. Some awesome cornices can hang well into summer just right of where the trail ascends.

North Arapaho Peak is seven-tenths of a mile to the north via a broken ridge. The route is marked with arrows and stays essentially on top of the ridge. While the route is not unduly

11

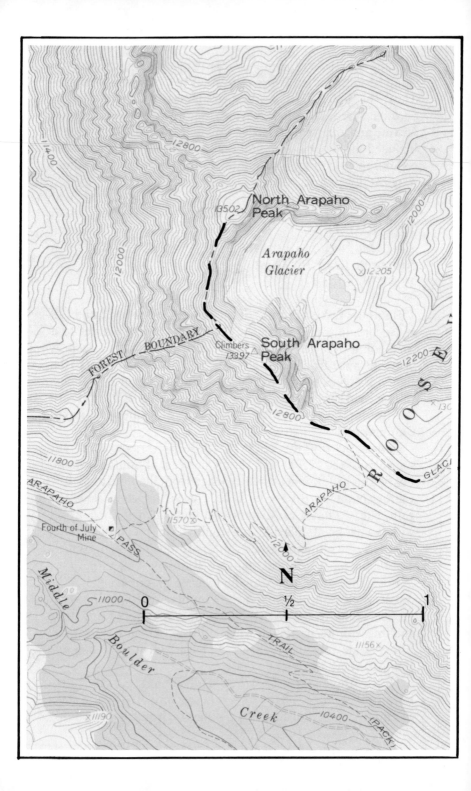

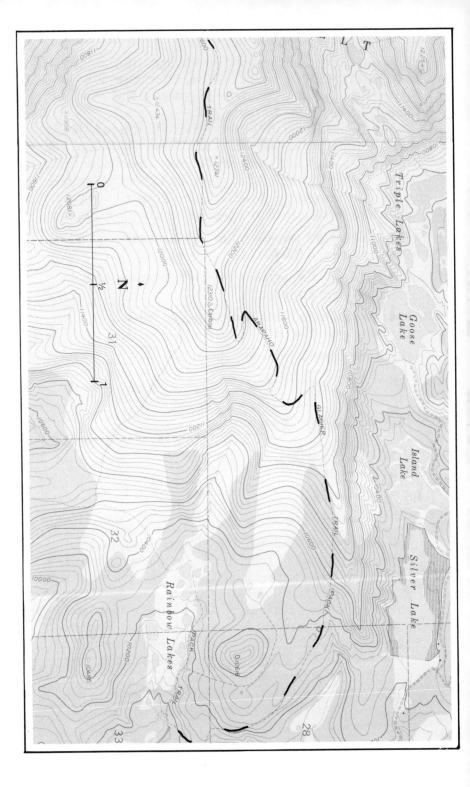

difficult, it does require some bouldering with considerable exposure, particularly to the east, where the ridge looks down on Arapaho Glacier. The ridge is generally fine rock, with handholds appearing where needed.

For the final climb to North Arapaho Peak, if snow blocks the main couloir, an alternate is to traverse slightly west and then up the backside (north side) of the summit ridge to the summit plateau. A return along the ridge to South Arapaho is necessary because the Boulder Water District heavily fines anyone trespassing in the drainage east and north of the peaks.

Rainbow Lakes Campground to South Arapaho: 6.5 miles
Elevation gain: 4,500 feet

Fourth of July Campground to South Arapaho: 4.5 miles
Elevation gain: 4,300 feet

South Arapaho to North and return: 1.4 miles
Elevation gain: 500 feet

(Route description from July climb)

JAMES PEAK
13,294 Feet
Front Range

If Edwin James had had a good press agent, perhaps his name, and not that of Zebulon Pike, would be memorialized on America's most famous mountain. In 1820, as a member of Stephen Long's expedition to the "Snowy Mountains," James, already a respected botanist, became a noted mountaineer by making the first recorded ascent of a Colorado Fourteener. Major Long sought to bestow James's name on the towering peak, but common usage by mountain men and fur traders preserved Pike's name on the mountain.

Edwin James, however, was not forgotten in the Colorado landscape. Botanist-turned-mountaineer, Dr. Charles C.

Looking west from I-70 at Genesee, James Peak is distinguishable by its impressive east face to the north of Parry Peak.

Parry placed James's name as well as his own on the twin summits astride the Continental Divide above Middle Park. When viewed from the Genessee Bridge on I-70, Parry Peak and its neighbor to the north, James Peak, are a dramatic view of the inner Rockies.

Shortly after Parry's visit in the early 1860s, Andrews N. Rogers, an eminent mining engineer and mayor of Central City, the boisterous mining town which boomed along the rocky banks of North Clear Creek just east of the peak, suggested a novel idea. Since railroads were being thwarted in their attempts to cross the rugged Continental Divide west of Denver, why not pierce the Divide with a tunnel beneath James Peak?

Such an idea! By 1904, however, David H. Moffat Jr.'s Denver, Northwestern, and Pacific Railroad had pushed its standard gauge rails across neighboring Rollins Pass, setting an altitude record of 11,671 feet, which stood until the line was abandoned in 1937. The abandonment, of course, was occasioned by the fulfillment of Rogers's idea. In 1928, the 6.2-mile-long Moffat Tunnel had been completed beneath the Divide just to the north of James Peak and Rogers Pass. With the completion of the Dotsero Cutoff in 1934, Denver at last had a direct rail line west to Salt Lake City. Perhaps even more important to Denver today than the railroad cars rumbling beneath James Peak is the Western Slope water that the Denver Water Board gathers from the Fraser River and sends eastward through the pioneer bore of the Moffat Tunnel.

While James Peak is a frequent family climb, its imposing east face offers a difficult technical challenge. Mountaineering historian Bill Bueler reports in *Roof of the Rockies* that Kenneth Segerstrom and Carleton Long made what was probably a first ascent of the east face in June of 1933 via the middle couloir.

THE ROUTES
Arapaho National Forest
Empire 7½ Quad
East Portal 7½ Quad

Jim Creek: From the four-way intersection at the main entrance to the Winter Park Ski Area on U.S. 40, three miles south of Winter Park, take the east fork, a dirt road leading northeast past green-colored residence and service buildings belonging to the Denver Water Board. Almost immediately the road forks. Take the east (right) fork and continue one-half mile to another fork. Again, take the east (right) fork and proceed generally east 1.7 miles along the Moffat Tunnel Diversion Ditch. Here, at a headgate, the road loops southwest back down the valley.

Park and hike up an old logging road along the south side of Jim Creek. The logging road soon becomes a trail, but after

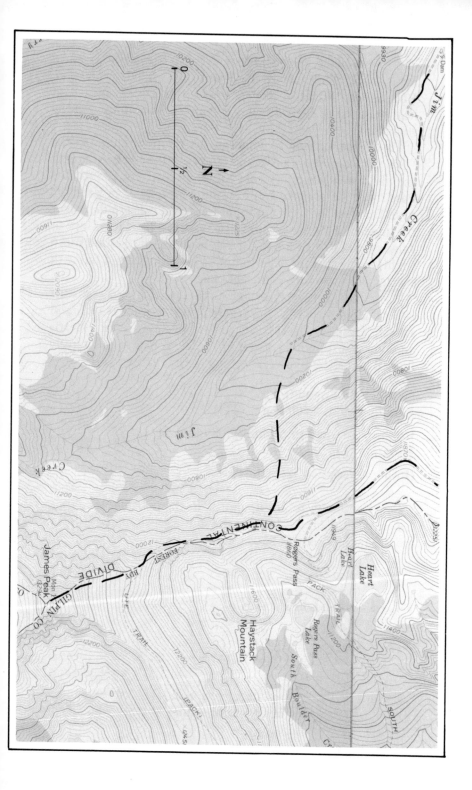

almost two miles, the trail becomes faint. Cross Jim Creek to the east and climb toward the depression in the ridge marking Rogers Pass. Either at Rogers Pass or just to the south of it near the crest of the ridge line, a trail leads south toward the summit.

Those not wishing to undergo the rigors of climbing the 1,800 vertical feet of timber and talus from the creek to the trail can also reach this point from Riflesight Notch on the Rollins Pass road. Simply hike south from the Notch two miles to the pass. Once on the trail, continue south just beneath the top of the ridge until the trail swings east across the northern slope of James Peak. From here it is a 900-foot, half-mile climb south (right) to the summit. The summit area is broad and flat with spectacular views down the east face.

If one descends back to Jim Creek, take care to cross the creek high in the basin. In early season Jim Creek is swift and swollen, and at least one golden retriever (who pleads anonymity with embarrassed brown eyes) had to be literally floated across by one very wet and angry master.

Headgate to Summit: 4 miles
Elevation gain: 4,000 feet

Rollins Pass road to Summit: 3.5 miles
Elevation gain: 2,200 feet

(Route description from July climb)

Other common routes up James Peak are from St. Mary's Glacier via the broad slopes of the southeast shoulder or from the old mining roads above Central City.

PETTINGELL PEAK
13,553 Feet
Front Range

Pettingell Peak owes its inclusion in this list to Mount Zirkel, or more specifically, to brooding weather which kept

Rocky point on
Pettingell ridge,
which drops sharply
to the north.

Looking west up Pettingell Peak's east ridge.

one guidebook author closer to home than he would have wished. Nonetheless, Pettingell Peak, particularly its steep north face, has definite class, coupled with a close proximity to the metropolitan Denver area.

Pettingell Peak is the high point of the peaks along the Continental Divide as it runs north from Loveland Pass toward Middle Park. To the south of Pettingell Peak, Hagar Mountain, 13,195 feet, and Citadel Peak, 13,294 feet, with its impressive northeast face, are particularly prominent.

Pettingell Peak was originally called Ptarmigan Peak. Erl and Scotty Ellis report in *The Saga of Upper Clear Creek* that it was renamed by the Forest Service in 1942 to honor Judge J.N. Pettingell of Hot Sulphur Springs. If the prospect hole high on the east ridge is any indication, the first ascent of the peak was probably made by miners.

THE ROUTES
Arapaho National Forest
Loveland Pass 7½ Quad
Grays Peak 7½ Quad

Herman Lake: From three miles west of Bakerville on I-70, exit north (right) and double back east along a dirt service road to the Herman Gulch trailhead (this is also the trailhead for Watrous Gulch). The Herman Gulch Trail forks west (left) several hundred yards from the parking area. Hike north and northwest for three miles to Herman Lake.

Pettingell Peak is directly northwest of the lake and offers two obvious routes. The less imaginative climbs directly northwest from the lake up several grassy steps and a large boulder field of moderate talus and then north (right) a short scramble to the summit. But by far the more interesting route is to climb directly north from the lake to a prominent saddle, from which a wide, sandy couloir descends, and then to follow the peak's east ridge west one-half mile to the summit.

From the lake the ridge appears quite broken, but the rock is generally stable with cuts or points offering adequate handholds, obstacles that may be easily skirted to the south

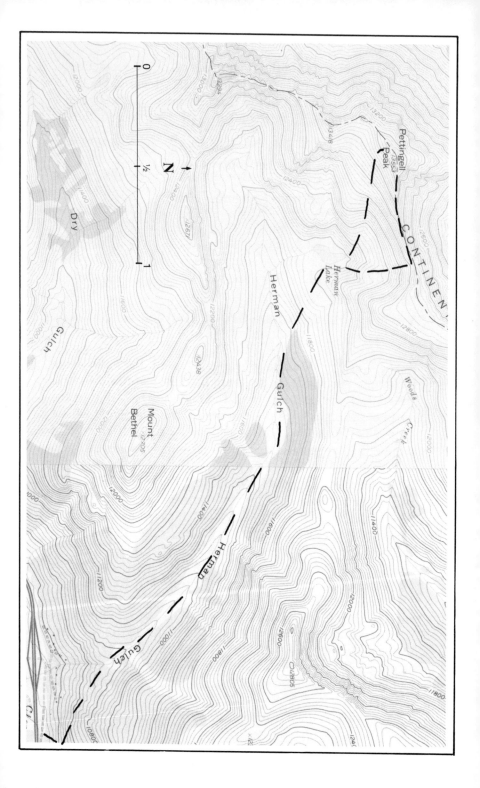

(left). The north side of this ridge drops off quite spectacularly. The summit view features Mount Powell, identifiable by its prominent flat summit in the Gore Range to the west, and a fine view of the north ridge of Torreys Peak to the southeast.

Trailhead to summit, either route: 4 miles
Elevation gain: 3,300 feet
(Route description from September climb)

BYERS PEAK
12,804 Feet
Vasquez Mountains—Front Range

The Vasquez Mountains snuggle up to Berthoud Pass, forming a portion of the southern boundary of Middle Park. Byers Peak stands apart from the main range, rising to the north of the high plateaus along which the Continental Divide runs west for a short distance. Its long north ridge and symmetrical appearance make it a prominent landmark from Middle Park.

Byers Peak was named by the Hayden Survey for William N. Byers, the intrepid founder and early editor of the *Rocky Mountain News*. Born in Ohio and educated as a surveyor, Byers arrived in Denver during the Pike's Peak Gold Rush, and early in 1859, he beat John Merrick's *Cherry Creek Pioneer* off the press by one day to make the *News* the first newspaper published in what was known as Denver City, Kansas.

In addition to his newspaper interests, Byers was also an energetic businessman. He was among the Denver visionaries who urged the engineer Edward Berthoud to find a pass through the mountains for a railroad. Byers later became closely tied to a variety of business interests in Middle Park, including the development of Hot Sulphur Springs, an early mountain resort.

Even without these accomplishments, Byers is deserving of

Byers Peak is a straightforward family climb with a trail which climbs its north ridge to the summit.

recognition on a prominent mountain because of his pioneer role in early Colorado mountaineering. John Wesley Powell, largely because of his subsequent achievements, is honored as the leader of the first known ascent of Longs Peak, but it was Byers who had attempted the climb four years earlier and who joined Powell in the first successful ascent.

Byers reached the summit of Longs Peak again in 1873 with the Hayden Survey, after joining its members in a number of possible first ascents, including Teocalli, La Plata, and Snowmass peaks. Finally, it was Byers who gave liberal editorial room to report the accomplishments of Major Powell, the Hayden and Wheeler surveys, and other climbing achievements.

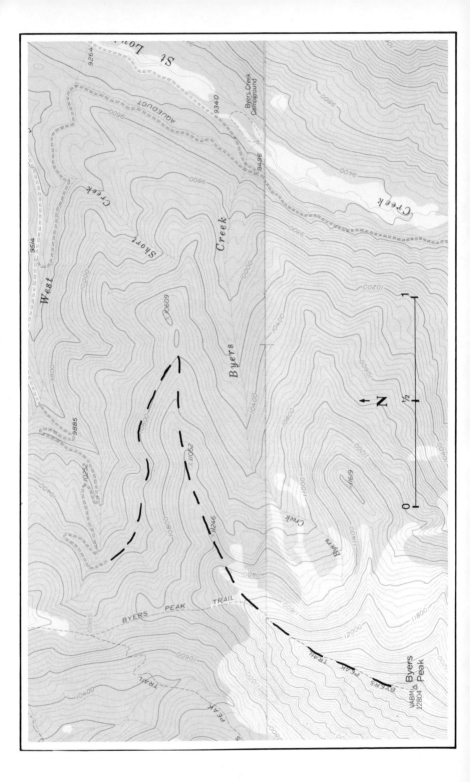

THE ROUTES
Arapaho National Forest
Bottle Pass 7½ Quad
Byers Peak 7½ Quad

West St. Louis Creek: Byers Peak is an easy family climb that offers fine views of the Gore Range and the frequently overlooked mountains near Loveland Pass. From Fraser on U.S. 40, proceed west on Eisenhower Drive, at the corner with the New Fraser Market. After several blocks, cross the railroad tracks, turn left immediately, and follow the road that goes south several blocks and then turns west to run up St. Louis Creek. (The whole Fraser area is undergoing rapid change, and finding your way out of town may be the most difficult part of the trip!)

Follow the St. Louis Creek Road, which may be marked with signs to the Fraser Experimental Forest, for a total of 12.5 miles to the trailhead. You will pass the St. Louis Creek Campground at mile 2.8, the headquarters of the Fraser Experimental Forest at 5.0, a tight turn back to the north just beyond the Byers Creek Campground at mile 7.6, and a seemingly endless set of switchbacks en route.

From the trailhead, the peak is a straight-forward hike along a trail that leads first east and then back to the west, gaining the peak's north ridge at timberline. (This trail is not the Byers Peak Trail shown on the accompanying map.) From timberline, the trail leads south approximately one mile to the summit. While the trail is easy, this ridge sometimes has massive snow cornices early in the season. On the descent, avoid the temptation to cut the long easterly switchback; doing so saves little time and disturbs fragile ecosystems.

Trailhead to summit: 3 miles
Elevation gain: 2,300 feet
(Route description from August climb)

SQUARE TOP MOUNTAIN
13,794 Feet
Front Range

The inclusion of Square Top Mountain in this selection of peaks stems not so much from any dramatic or unique qualities of its own, but rather from the interesting view from the summit. To the east are Mount Evans and Mount Bierstadt, connected by the impressive Sawtooth. To the south unfolds the broad expanse of South Park. To the northwest rise Grays and Torreys peaks above valleys which once resounded with the clamor of frenzied mining activity.

Square Top Mountain is easily recognized to the west of Guanella Pass by its prominent east cirque.

North from Square Top, across the saddle between Argentine Peak and Mount Wilcox (easily recognizable as the route of a major power line) is the Leavenworth Creek valley. There, the town of Waldorf and the Santiago Mine were once so promising that in 1906 a Methodist minister, Edward John Wilcox, completed the famed Argentine Central Railway to link them with Silver Plume. Revenues from hauling silver ore were disappointing, but the narrow gauge line was popular with turn-of-the-century tourists, who thrilled at the Shay locomotives puffing their way up McClellan Mountain.

South of McClellan Mountain, hidden from the Square Top view by Argentine Peak, is Argentine Pass, at 13,207 feet, the site of the highest road crossing the Continental Divide. It was built as a toll road in 1871 by the colorful "Commodore" Stephen Decatur to connect Georgetown on the east with the silver mines of Peru Creek and Horseshoe Basin on the west. The steep western side of the pass, once a terrifying descent in a wagon laden with goods, is impassable to vehicles.

Square Top's first ascent was undoubtedly by Indians or miners. It makes a good beginner or family climb with a touch of history thrown in for spice.

THE ROUTES
Arapaho National Forest
Montezuma 7½ Quad
Mount Evans 7½ Quad

Guanella Pass: From Georgetown, drive south on the Guanella Pass road for ten miles to the parking area atop the pass at 11,669 feet. While the crowds head east to tackle Mount Bierstadt, hike west toward Square Top, which is easily recognized by the impressive cirque on its east face. This is a moderate hike providing parties stay on the ridges and avoid the cirque or the talus of the north face. Two routes are easily distinguishable. One leads across a scattering of willows (nothing compared to the infamous Bierstadt willows across the road) to the gently sloping ridge running north from the flat saddle above Square Top Lakes. Follow the ridge over the

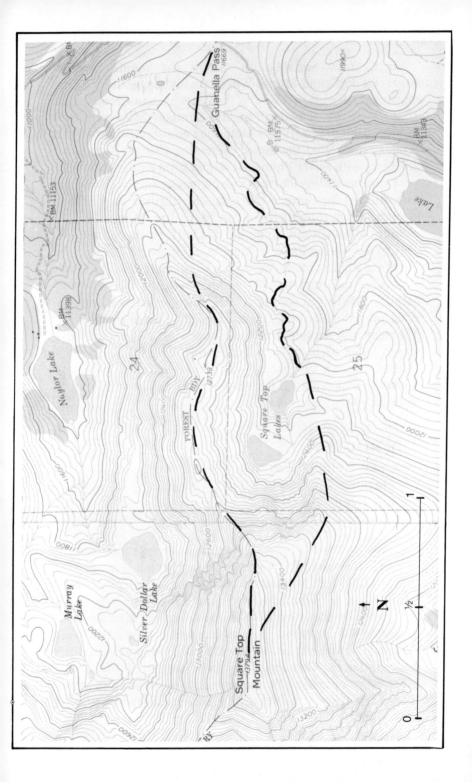

12,739-foot point, around the head of Square Top Lakes Basin, and up a short section of steep scrambling to the final summit ridge.

The other route loses several hundred feet of elevation by following a series of old roads into Square Top Lakes Basin and then loops south onto the broad southeast shoulder, avoiding the cirque. Square Top makes an interesting winter climb, but the Guanella Pass area is extremely dangerous avalanche terrain, and parties should exercise great care in route selection.

Guanella Pass to summit: 3 miles
Elevation gain: 2,125 feet
(Route description from October climb)

A longer route to Square Top starts from the Naylor Lake turnoff at the abrupt curve about one and one-half miles north of Guanella Pass. The enterprising can pick routes up to the 12,739-foot point described above or head west into the basin of Murray and Silver Dollar lakes and reach the saddle between Square Top and Argentine Peak. The cliffs immediately south of Silver Dollar Lake should be avoided.

MOUNT ROSALIE
13,575 Feet
Front Range

Mount Rosalie is the rounded hump on the southeastern flank of the Mount Evans massif and is quite prominent from metropolitan Denver. The mountain makes a good early season conditioner or late fall hike—thereby avoiding the midsummer autos chugging along on nearby Mount Evans.

During the initial mining rush of 1859, the entire Mount Evans massif was known as the Chicago Mountains. Then in 1863, Albert Bierstadt, the soon-to-be-reknowned western

Mount Rosalie looking west up the drainage of Deer Creek from U.S. 285.

landscape painter, and Fitz-Hugh Ludlow, a writer for the *Atlantic Monthly*, passed through Denver en route to Yosemite and the Northwest. Ludlow wrote in the *Atlantic* that they bestowed the name "Rosalie" on the mountain after "a dear absent friend of mine and Bierstadt's." This was a reference to Rosalie Osbourne of Waterville, New York, who later married Ludlow. She was also a good friend of Bierstadt's, however, for after Ludlow's death, Bierstadt married her. Rosalie shared in Bierstadt's tours until her death in 1893.

Bierstadt may have made the first ascent of "Mount Rosalie" with William N. Byers during that early trip in 1863 or possibly on a later journey in 1866. In any event, Bierstadt's "Mount Rosalie" served as the subject for his famous "Storm in the Rocky Mountains." During the next few years, the name

"Rosalie" went through several corruptions due in part to writings which found the massif to be similar to Monte Rosa in the Alps.

By 1870, however, this highest peak west of Denver had been christened Mount Evans, in honor of second territorial governor and railroader John Evans. This act was officially ratified by the state legislature in 1895, and the name "Rosalie" began a journey first to present Mount Epaulet, then to present Mount Bierstadt, and finally to its current resting place on the rounded hump which forms the southern end of the Evans massif.

THE ROUTES
Arapaho National Forest
Harris Park 7½ Quad

Tanglewood Creek: From U.S. 285 between Bailey and Pine Junction, near the top of Crow Hill, turn west and follow Park County 43 northwest up Deer Creek for 6.8 miles. Here, the road forks, with the west (left) fork leading another 1.3 miles to Deer Creek Campground. At the campground take the north (right) fork another mile, past summer cottages, to the Deer Creek trailhead at 9,248 feet. Hike west from the parking area, immediately taking the north (right) fork of the trail marked "Tanglewood Creek." Continue north on the trail (staying to the right at several junctions with side trails) for almost two and one-half miles until at a large marsh Tanglewood Creek veers west. Here, the trail continues north for another half-mile to a timberline of bristlecone pines. Continue north to the saddle just west of the Pegmatite Points and then west another mile and a half up gentle slopes to the rounded summit.

This route makes a fine ski approach, as was necessary when I climbed it one snowy May, with only slight difficulty in the steep and heavily timbered terrain between the marsh and timberline. Winter or summer, persons who stray from the trail will find that whoever named Tanglewood Creek had indeed been there.

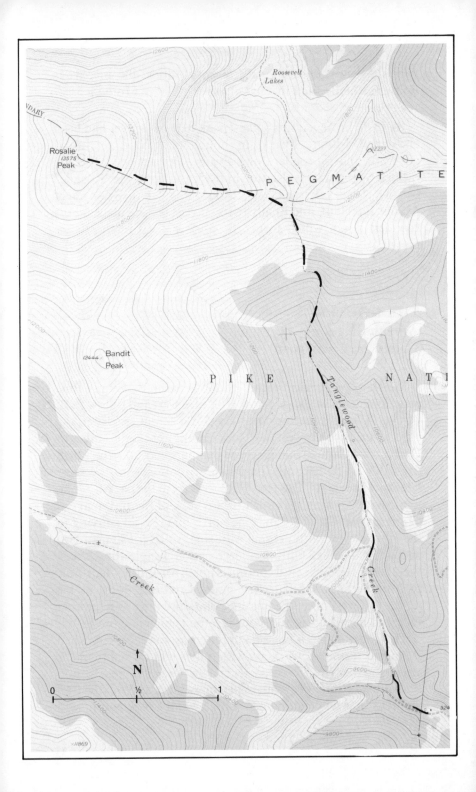

Trailhead to summit: 4.5 miles
Elevation Gain: 4,350 feet
(Route description from May climb)

Mount Rosalie can also be reached from the main Deer Creek Trail and from Bandit Peak or from the Rosalie and Scott Gomer trails to the southwest. Summer climbs from the Mount Evans highway are less than sporting.

MOUNT GUYOT
13,370 Feet
Front Range

Mount Guyot, a French name pronounced "ghee-yo," is the prominent point straight ahead as one descends the west side of Kenosha Pass on U.S. 285. The mountain is equally striking to the north of Bald Peak, when viewed across Lake Dillon from the Frisco overlook on I-70. Guyot is a short family climb when the Georgia Pass road is open or offers some possibilities for longer ascents in winter or early spring.

Mount Guyot is one of the peaks that Charles C. Parry, our ubiquitous botanist and explorer, named for scientific colleagues. (*See* Mount Audubon.) Parry named this mountain in honor of Arnold H. Guyot (1807-1884), a Swiss-born naturalist, geologist, and textbook author, who enjoyed a distinguished career in the geology department of Princeton University.

Some arduous research by Mike Foster of the Colorado Mountain Club's *Trail and Timberline* staff turned up an interesting coincidence between Arnold Guyot and the geologic term "guyot," which refers to a submerged oceanic volcano whose summit has been worn flat by wave action. Despite the flat appearance of Mount Guyot's summit, particularly when viewed from Frisco, the mountain was nonetheless named for Arnold Guyot and not for its resemblance to a submerged volcano. The geologic term

Mount Guyot presents a striking silhouette from just west of Kenosha Pass.

"guyot" did not appear until the 1940s, when long-time Princeton geology professor Harry Hess gave the name to the oceanic volcanos. Hess got his inspiration for the term from Princeton's Guyot Hall, which houses the Department of Geology and which, of course, was named for the University's famous nineteenth-century professor of geology—Arnold Guyot!

The famed explorer John C. Fremont passed to the west of Mount Guyot in June of 1844, while puzzling over the geography of the central Rockies. Fremont avoided the Indian trail across the pass north of Guyot into South Park because of roaming Arapaho warriors, and instead, crossed Hoosier Pass into South Park. Fifteen years later, placer gold discoveries near Breckenridge started a flow of prospectors across what became Georgia Pass. The pass was the main route into Breckenridge, until replaced by the smoother grades of Hoosier and Boreas passes.

Mount Guyot's close proximity to the Georgia Pass road does not render it void of danger. The mountain's prominence on the western fringe of South Park is a fine place for thunderstorms to build. In August of 1981, four men were camping on the summit of Mount Guyot, when one of the tents was struck by lightning, electrocuting the two inside. Their two companions tried unsuccessfully to revive them and then went for help, but it was four days before rescuers could reach the summit through the ensuing storms. Both men were pronounced dead from cardiac arrest caused by the lightning bolts. One of the climbers who went for help also suffered burns on his feet from the lightning.

Mount Guyot is reached from the Georgia Pass Road and climbed either by its gentle east-sloping ridge or the right-hand skyline which runs southwest from the summit of Georgia Pass.

Summit ridge on Mount Guyot was heavily corniced and steeper than it looks here in June of 1982.

THE ROUTES
Arapaho National Forest
Boreas Pass 7½ Quad

  Michigan Creek/Georgia Pass Approach: From Jefferson on U.S. 285 north of Fairplay, drive west on the Jefferson Lake road. Continue west (straight) at mile 2 when the Jefferson Lake road turns north (right). Nine-tenths of a mile further, take the west (right) fork now marked as Park County 54 or Forest Service 400, and continue almost three miles to a fork. From here, some confusion as to maps may exist. On the Forest Service map, the main road is the southwest (left) fork leading first one-half mile to Michigan Creek Campground and then three miles up first French Creek and then back to

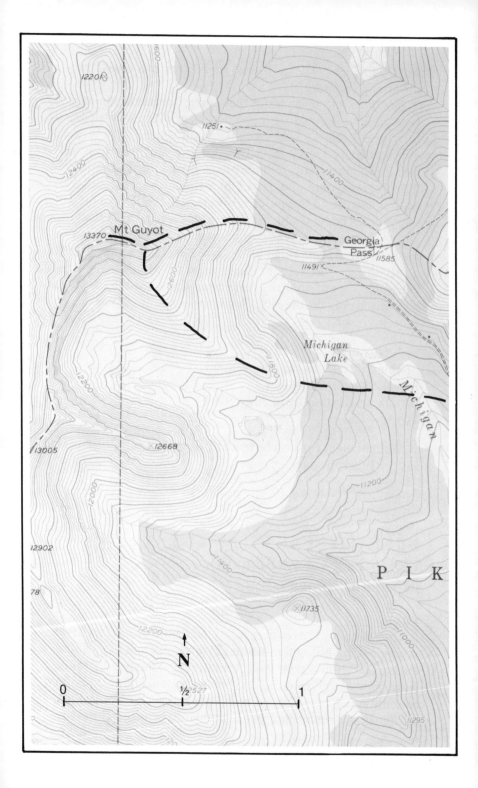

12201

1600

11251

12400

11400

Mt Guyot

13370

Georgia
Pass

11585

11491

12600

Michigan
Lake

11800

Michigan

13005

12200

12668

11200

12902

11400

P I K

78

11735

12200

N

1000

0   ½ 2527   1

11295

Michigan Creek. The northwest (right) fork continues straight up Michigan Creek.

For the climb to be more than a stroll from the summit of Georgia Pass (providing it is open), park where the left-hand fork (the French Creek road) crosses Michigan Creek at approximately 11,100 feet. This is about a quarter of a mile west of the two roads rejoining each other. From here, climb directly west onto the broad but steep southeast ridge of Mount Guyot and follow it northwest to the summit, a total of two miles. The final summit ridge drops sharply to both sides and may be corniced early in the season. The descent can be made down the east ridge to Georgia Pass with some glissade possibilities. The cirque due south of Mount Guyot is extremely rugged, and the more adventuresome may want to try their hands on the ridge from the point at 12,668 feet to Mount Guyot.

Michigan Creek to summit: 2 miles
Elevation gain: 2,300 feet
(Route description from June climb)

Mount Guyot can also be reached via the French Gulch road east of Breckenridge.

BUFFALO PEAKS
13,326 Feet (West Summit)
Mosquito Range

The Buffalo Peaks are easily recognizable as the two prominent ant hills guarding the southwestern exit from South Park over Trout Creek Pass. Undoubtedly, Juan Bautista de Anza saw them in 1779 as he led his band of Spanish conquistadors over Trout Creek Pass and across South Park on the first documented penetration of the inner Colorado

Buffalo Peaks looking south from just west of the described trailhead.

Rockies by Europeans. Twenty-seven years later, a bewildered Zebulon Pike crossed Trout Creek Pass into the Arkansas Valley in time to spend a frigid Christmas beneath Mount Shavano.

When the mining boom began in 1859, Weston Pass, long a Ute trail north of the peaks, became a key route from South Park into the upper Arkansas Valley. The pass's gentle slopes and the headwaters of the South Fork of the South Platte River cut the Buffalo Peaks off from the main Mosquito Range and offer an easier and lower route across the range than Mosquito Pass to the north. Traffic over Weston Pass declined after construction crews of the Denver South Park and Pacific

Heading south toward East Buffalo Peak with one "straggler" turning back to check on the photographer.

Railroad laid narrow gauge rails past the Buffalo Peaks in 1880 en route to Leadville and the mining camps in the Gunnison country.

Geologically, the Buffalo Peaks are a remnant of layers of lava and volcanic ash. The saddle connecting the peaks is impressively steep on the north side and offers a rugged backdrop to the Lynch Creek Basin. Aside from the expanse of South Park unfolding to the east, the summit view is intriguing because it features the military-like line-up of the Sawatch Range—neat and orderly, one mountain after another—across the Arkansas Valley to the west. The valley itself appears particularly wide and flat, an impression one does not get when driving through it.

THE ROUTES
Pike National Forest
Marmot Peak 7½ Quad
Jones Hill 7½ Quad

Buffalo Springs Access Road: From Fairplay, drive thirteen miles south, or from Antero Junction, drive nine miles north on U.S. 285 to Forest Service 431. From 285, drive west over a dusty but moderate dirt road past the Buffalo Springs Campground, Long Park, and Willow Creek, approximately nine miles to a junction just prior to reaching a large meadow. The west (right) fork leads through the meadow and then deadends, while the south (left) fork is blocked by a gate. Hike up the south fork, an old logging trail, generally east and above

Looking west toward West Buffalo Peak and the impressive colonnades at the head of the Lynch Creek Basin.

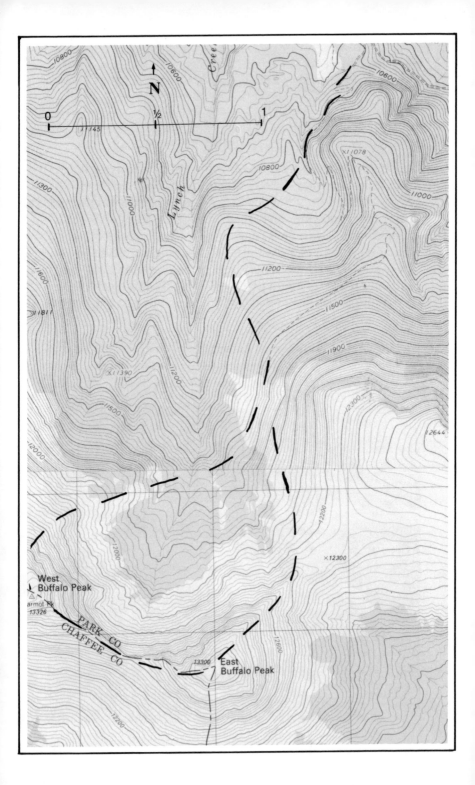

the drainage of Lynch Creek toward the basin between the peaks. A series of logging trails criss-cross and can cause some confusion. Stay on the main trail or, if enticed onto a logging trail, keep bearing generally south and higher in elevation. The principal logging trail emerges from the trees after about two and one-half miles and climbs the broad northeast ridge of East Buffalo Peak. Angle for the point at the base of the summit ridge, at 12,450 feet, then scramble up a moderate ridge to the summit.

In contrast to the football field smoothness of the northeast flank below the 12,450-foot point, the wall forming the head of the Lynch Creek Basin is a series of impressive cliffs and volcanic palisades coming off West Buffalo Peak to the saddle. The summits of both peaks are large and flat, and each looks higher when viewed from the other.

The traverse is easy scrambling several feet to the south of the crest. From West Buffalo Peak, descend north down a broad ridge, staying to the west (left) of the cliffs on the east face. Either continue north down the ridge and across a burn area and Lynch Creek to the meadow parking or traverse east fairly high in the valley down a loosely timbered slope to reach the logging trails below the ascent route. In either case, it is important to cross Lynch Creek to the east well above the elevation of the meadow parking area.

Meadow to summits with traverse and return: 10 miles
Elevation gain: 3,700 feet (including 550-foot drop to saddle)
(Route description from June climb)

8-15-2000

TENMILE PEAK
12,933 Feet
Tenmile Range

The Tenmile Range is a twelve-mile chain of interesting summits serving as a north-south link to connect the Gore and

43

Looking east to Tenmile Peak. The summit is behind the snowy point.

Mosquito ranges. To the east, the range drops moderately to the Blue River, but on the west the vertical walls of Tenmile Canyon are a testament to the awesome sculpture of ancient glaciers.

The range is numbered from north to south, Peak One through Peak Ten, followed by the more imaginative names of Crystal, Pacific, Fletcher, and Quandary. Tenmile Peak takes the place of Peak Two in the chronology, presumably because it is the high point of the northern section of the range.

Explorer John C. Fremont first skirted the Tenmile Range in 1844 while hurrying over Hoosier Pass en route to St. Louis, and then again in 1845 while crossing Tennessee Pass bound for California. Fremont missed the pass, then known as Arkansas Pass, which today honors him.

According to Tenmile historians Stan Dempsey and Jay Fell, the Tenmile name derives from what early miners thought was the approximate distance from Breckenridge to the confluence of Blue River and Tenmile Creek, a place which today lies beneath the waters of Lake Dillon. Miners probably made the first ascent of Tenmile Peak and most of the others in the range.

Both the Denver and Rio Grande Railway and the Denver South Park and Pacific Railroad tackled the rocky walls of Tenmile Canyon to tap the mining boom. The Rio Grande eventually reached Dillon after building over Fremont Pass from Leadville. When blocked by the Rio Grande from expanding its line near Buena Vista direct to Leadville, the South Park built over Boreas Pass first to Breckenridge, then to Frisco, and finally over Fremont Pass to Leadville.

"Get serious! Is this really June 4th?" Vic Rosengren on a "winter" attempt at Tenmile Peak.

The impressive "Tooth" south of the summit of Tenmile Peak.

THE ROUTES
Arapaho National Forest
Frisco 7½ Quad
Vail Pass 7½ Quad

Miners Creek: From the intersection of Main Street and Colorado 9 in downtown Frisco, drive south and east one-half mile to a paved road heading south at the Highway Department garage. Continue straight on this road, which becomes dirt when the pavement curves left to the county shops, one-half mile to a junction which may also be reached directly from Colorado 9 just beyond the Highway Department garage. From the junction, drive south one-half mile to Rainbow Lake Campground and another three miles to the trailhead or as far as is passable in cars. Usually, two-wheel drives last for only one to two miles depending on the season. There are numerous intersections on this road; however, most lead to the trailhead if one continues generally southwest.

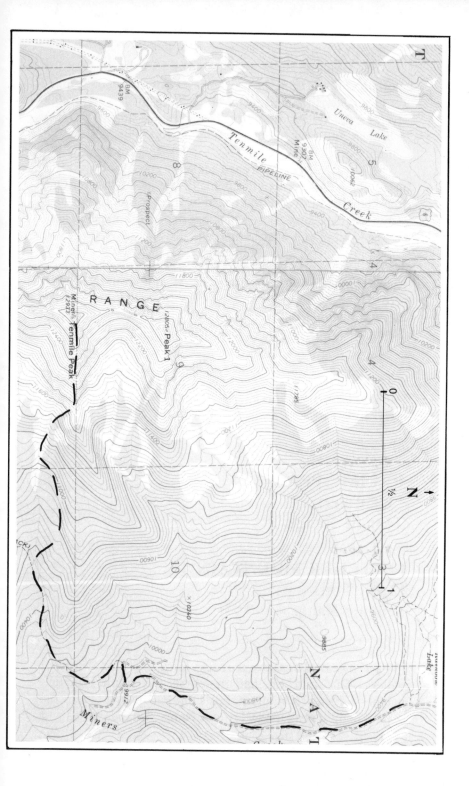

At the trailhead, hike west along Miner's Creek Trail for another half-mile until the trail emerges in a wide marshy area. Tenmile Peak is visible directly west. Climb northwest through several small valleys mounting Tenmile's east ridge. The ridge is broken and rocky, but a moderate scramble west to the summit.

The Miner's Creek approach makes a good winter ski trip although avalanche conditions may preclude an ascent. One June climb by this route was foiled by three to four feet of corn snow—that special variety which has one constantly changing between skiing and post-holing.

Approximate end for passenger cars (1 mile from trailhead) to summit: 2.5 miles
Elevation gain: 3,100 feet
(Route description from August climb)

Tenmile Peak may also be approached from Officers Gulch Campground in Tenmile Canyon via a much steeper and more direct route.

8-15-2000
PACIFIC PEAK
13,950 Feet
Tenmile Range

8-2-2000
FLETCHER MOUNTAIN
13,951 Feet
Tenmile Range

Pacific Peak rises above the rocky terraces of glacial-scarred valleys. One and one-half miles to the south, Pacific's neighbor, Fletcher Montain, beats out Pacific by a foot as the second highest peak in the Tenmile Range. Quandary Peak, at

Pacific Peak looking northeast from the Mayflower Gulch road.

Craig Koontz ascending the final west summit ridge on Pacific Peak with the Mayflower Gulch drainage in the background.

14,265 feet, is the high point of the range, and when viewed from Pacific and Fletcher mountains, its rugged north and west sides form a sharp contrast to the long, sloping east ridge by which the mountain is usually climbed.

Between Pacific Peak and Fletcher Mountain is a 13,841-foot point which is one of ten unnamed summits in the list of Colorado's 100 highest peaks. Between this point and Fletcher Mountain lies a serrated ridge of pinnacles that Bob Ormes called appropriately "the rock fountain." It forms the head of the beautiful Mayflower Creek amphitheater.

The first ascents of both Pacific and Fletcher peaks may well have been by miners or perhaps by Indians who valued the mountains as scouting points above the trails into South Park. Because of the extensive mining activity and the relative narrowness of the range, the surveys paid little attention to the Tenmile Peaks, preferring instead to concentrate on the lure of Mount of the Holy Cross and other unknowns. At some early time, however, the name Pacific was bestowed, probably in reference to its stand near the dividing point between the headwaters of the Arkansas River flowing east toward the Atlantic Ocean and the creeks flowing west toward the Pacific Ocean. Fletcher seems to have been the name of an early miner.

Mining activity was extensive both in the vicinity of Breckenridge, along the Blue River to the east of the mountains, and north of Fremont Pass along Tenmile Creek west of the range. Placer mining began along both watercourses in the early 1860s, but the boom was short-lived, and attempts to extract gold and silver from the region's complex ore failed for lack of adequate technology. By 1879, however, a new boom was on and the towns of Robinson and Kokomo

Fletcher Peak in the background looking northwest up the approach drainage from Blue Lakes Reservoir.

were thriving just north of Fremont Pass. Their ruins now lie beneath the gray sludge of the Climax tailings ponds.

Although not nearly as extensive as the workings west of Tenmile Creek, some mining was done high in the valleys beneath Pacific Peak and Fletcher Mountain. At the center of Mayflower Gulch are the ruins of Boston, founded in the early 1900s to support the work of the Boston Mining Company. The work which went on there with pick and shovel eventually gave way to a different style of mining several ridges to the south. The metal there was molybdenum, and giant shovels replaced the miner's pick.

THE ROUTES
Arapaho National Forest
Copper Mountain 7½ Quad
Breckenridge 7½ Quad

Pacific Peak-Mayflower Gulch/Boston: From the junction of I-70 and Colorado 91 at Copper Mountain, drive south on Colorado 91 five and one-half miles, or from the summit of Fremont Pass at Climax drive north on Colorado 91 five and one-half miles, to an unmarked turnoff and large asphalt parking area on the east side of the highway. This is the access road up Mayflower Creek. While the road is passable in vehicles, the land is private, and the owner restricts access to foot traffic only.

From the parking area, hike southeast up the access road one and one-half miles to the remains of Boston. The road stays to the south (right) of the creek, and while the Pacific Creek drainage becomes readily visible, the walk to Boston is more pleasant than striking out directly for Pacific Creek across a broad patch of willows.

At Boston, turn north (left) across the head of the willows and angle slightly back down the valley, making for a trail which runs just to the west (left) of the large talus slope. This faint trail runs to a mine on the shoulder of the ridge forming the Pacific Creek Basin. From the mine, contour east (right) around the shoulder and into the glacial-scarred basin.

Amid the scree on the west ridge of Pacific Peak, a triangular patch of larger talus leads to the west ridge just east (right) of a rather prominent fin. The talus is generally stable, but there is some danger of rockfall. Once on the ridge, a small point must be passed either via a couloir to the north (left) or via a ledge and smaller couloir to the south (right). Here, the rock is very loose. Once atop this section, the ridge is a short scramble over larger talus until the final—and somewhat unexpected—thrill of finding a thirty-foot gash in the ridge just below the summit. It is easily negotiated to the south (right), but the dropoff to the north face is dramatic!

A descent route down the ridge to the southeast and then down a series of scree couloirs offers the best route back to the basin. In early season, experienced parties may benefit from snow on both ascent and descent.

Parking lot to summit: 3 miles
Elevation gain: 3,200 feet
(Route description from October climb)

(Incidentally, Colorado 91 has been moved east since this map was published, accounting for the discrepancy in map mileage and the lack of a parking area on the map.)

For those not interested in Pacific Peak's west ridge, there appears to be a route angling up toward the saddle between Pacific and the unnamed 13,841-foot point to the south. The rock looks equally loose, but once atop the saddle, there is a wide ridge to the summit from the southeast. This approach is also reached out of Breckenridge via McCullough Gulch.

Fletcher Mountain-Monte Cristo Creek: From eight miles south of Breckenridge on Colorado 9, drive west on Summit County Road 850 for 2.3 miles to Blue Lakes Dam or, in the spring, to the end of the plowed road. From the dam, follow a trail west beneath the prominent couloir descending from the summit of Quandary Peak. The trail is hard to find and requires climbing up several hundred feet of crumbling slopes

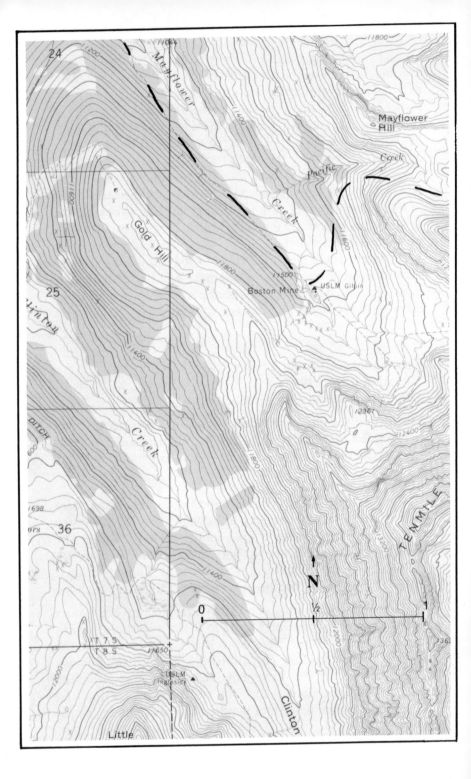

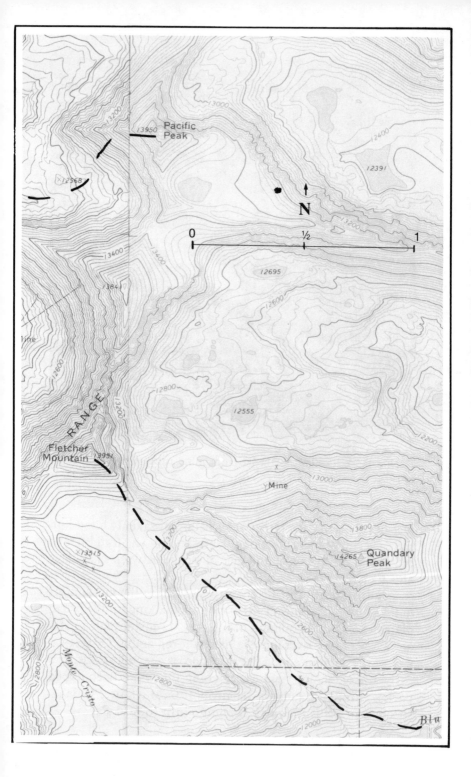

Pacific Peak looking northeast from mine ruins. *Craig F. Koontz photo.*

just beyond the dam rather than being mistakenly lured into the easier-looking route along the reservoir. The trail leads to old cabin ruins in the grand glacial cirque between Quandary and Fletcher peaks.

Continue northwest up the valley, skirting the minor cliffs halfway up the cirque on either side and making for the broad plateau beneath the summit of Fletcher. From the plateau, it is an easy scramble over loose talus up the remaining 700 vertical feet of the summit cone. The rock here is generally talus, and early season snows yield easier going for properly equipped parties. From the summit, the dropoff to Mayflower Gulch is spectacular, as is the ridge running north toward Pacific.

Fletcher Peak looking south over 13,841-foot point from Pacific. *Craig F. Koontz photo.*

Blue Lakes Dam to summit: 2 miles
Elevation gain: 2,200 feet

Colorado 9 to summit: 4.3 miles
Elevation gain: 3,150 feet

(Route description from July climb)

Like Pacific Peak, Fletcher Mountain can also be reached from Mayflower Gulch, but this entails either a tricky ridge climb over Fletcher's 13,880-foot southwest subpeak or tackling its crumbling west face head on.

MOUNT POWELL
13,534 Feet
Gore Range

Major John Wesley Powell was a man who truly deserved to have a rugged mountain named after him. In 1868, this intrepid, one-armed Civil War veteran spent a summer investigating the headwaters of the Grand River. On August 23, Powell led a party, which included William N. Byers of the *Rocky Mountain News*, to the summit of Longs Peak—the first recorded ascent of the mountain. The view of the river drainages to the west intrigued Powell, as did the range of craggy summits that he called the "Eagle River Range."

A month after the Longs Peak climb, on September 28, 1868, Powell and Ned E. Farrell, a college student and veteran of the Longs Peak venture, climbed the high point of the "Eagle River Range," making another first recorded ascent. Oramel G. Howland, then a correspondent for the *Rocky Mountain News*, accompanied the duo part of the way and referred to the peak in his report as Powell Mountain. Ned Farrell, in a dispatch to the *Chicago Tribune*, also called the peak Mount Powell and noted that the name was most appropriate "because the Major was the first to set foot on the summit." (Less than a year later, Powell made his famous voyage down the Colorado River. It was on this trip, deep in the depths of the Grand Canyon, that Howland and two others, disenchanted with the Major's leadership, left the main party and climbed out of the canyon, only to be killed by Paiute Indians.)

After Powell's group, the next mountaineers to reach the summit belonged to the Hayden Survey. The party included topographer James T. Gardner and Ferdinand Hayden himself. What a glorious time that climbing summer of 1873 must have been for the Hayden Survey! Its teams were just about everywhere, and Gardner climbed Mount Powell on August 28, just four days after the first known ascent of the Mount of the Holy Cross! Hayden described the surrounding "Blue River Range" as a "mass of sharp-pointed peaks, crests, and obelisks." Hayden found Powell's summit record and

The summit of Mount Powell lies to the north beyond the apparent high point here. Note the ledge ascending from the right.

fixed Powell's name on the mountain when he published the Hayden Atlas in 1877.

During the next sixty years, there were only two recorded ascents of Mount Powell—one in 1913 by Percy Hagerman of Pyramid Peak fame and one in 1931 by a survey team of the U.S. Geological Survey. Hagerman found Powell's summit record badly mutilated, but intact.

Finally, during the mid-1930s, the Colorado Mountain Club began to poke its way into the Gore Range, which became a popular climbing site. This late-blooming popularity was due to isolation, which as Bill Bueler rightly points out, is somewhat ironic because the most satisfying aspect of climbing in the Gore Range today is its isolation.

THE ROUTES
White River National Forest
Mount Powell 7½ Quad
Vail East 7½ Quad

The entire Gore Range is tough and rugged country, and Mount Powell is certainly no exception. This is a major mountain which should be approached with experience and caution. While the route described presents no technical difficulties, it can be particularly unpleasant in poor weather. The rugged terrain also requires careful route-finding.

Piney Lake Approach-South Face: From I-70 in Vail, take the main Vail exit, #176, and proceed west for one mile on the north service road that parallels the interstate. Turn north (right) on the Red Sandstone Creek Road. This road switchbacks above Vail and forks after .7 miles. Take the west (left) branch, which turns to gravel and goes north a total of 11.6 miles to Piney Lake. Take the west (left) fork at mile 3.4 and the north (right) fork at mile 7.4. At a small campground at mile 10, the road forks again, with the east (right) fork continuing 1.6 miles to Piney Lake.

Piney Lake Ranch is private property, and visitors must park outside the gate and use the wilderness area access trail which runs along the north side of the lake. Near the lake, the Sheephorn Trail forks north (left) and climbs the hillside. Continue up the main drainage along the Upper Piney Creek Trail. The trail crosses two side streams coming into Piney Creek from the north and then climbs through a series of rock outcrops.

Less than a quarter of a mile beyond the top of these outcrops, the main Upper Piney Trail continues east, while a faint and possibly hard to find trail angles northeast into the drainage beneath Mount Powell. This drainage empties into Upper Piney Creek where the main Upper Piney Trail curves sharply southeast, an easily recognizable point. If you reach this third side stream and the described point, you have gone beyond the trail junction and must either retrace your steps or bushwhack directly north up this drainage.

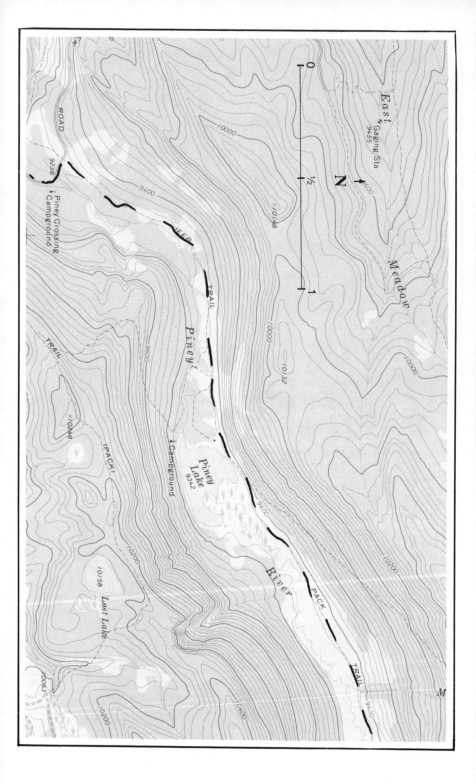

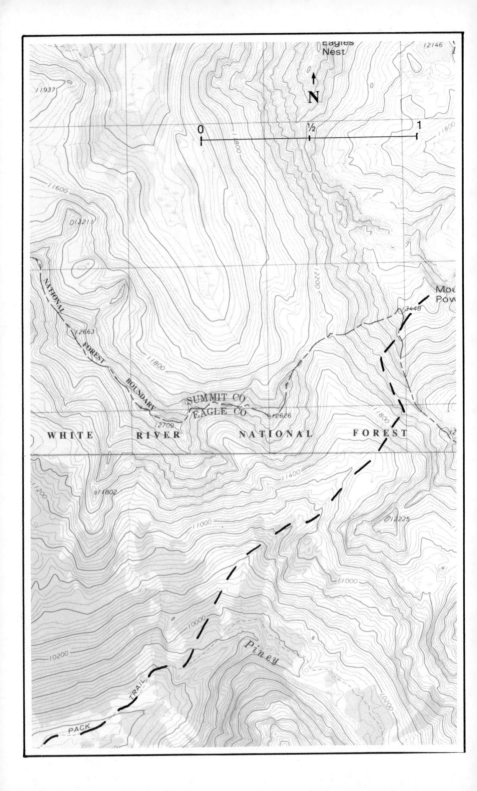

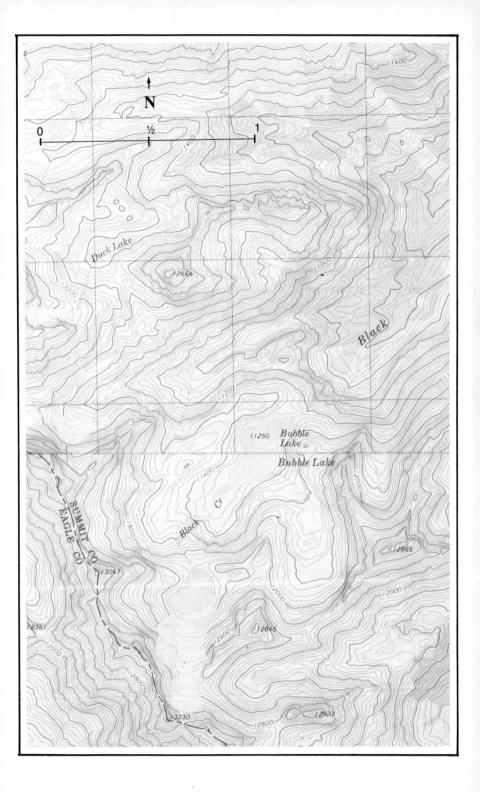

The side trail climbs northeasterly into the basin beneath Mount Powell. As you enter the basin, there is an ideal opportunity to scrutinize the route up the mountain. The large, tooth-shaped peak at the head of the valley is Peak C. To its left is a very prominent saddle with a couloir running down into the basin. Mount Powell lies to the left of the saddle, recognizable from here by several small points above the couloir and by three very prominent points between those and the summit. In the late summer a prominent green, grassy ledge can be seen cutting across the south face of the mountain. This ledge begins at the east (right) side of the peak and climbs west (left) to the prominent couloir running down from the notch between the summit plateau and the three major points noted above.

While it is possible to pick any number of routes up the south face, the grassy slopes are steep, the couloirs trashy, and the cliffs hazardous. One route which will work is to cross the basin directly below the south face and then climb toward the prominent grassy ledge. (There is a lower, less prominent grassy ledge which should be avoided.) After climbing the steepening, grassy slopes of the face, zig slightly east (right) in order to reach the desired main ledge. Follow this grassy ledge west (left) across the face of the mountain until it tops out overlooking the broad couloir running to the high saddle. This point is just above a prominent rock formation, most easily described as a big thumb, which should be noted to aid in route finding on the descent. Angle right and up amid loose scree into the higher reaches of this couloir, then climb to the small saddle at its head. Once atop the saddle, the summit is anticlimatic. Simply cross the flat summit plateau to the north and scramble up the remaining hundred feet of large boulders.

As the high point of the Gore Range, the view from Mount Powell's summit is particularly impressive. To the west is Meridian Peak, and to the north the long traverse to Eagle's Nest. Descend the same way, taking care to exit the broad couloir at "the thumb."

This route description is based on a September climb. Snow or rain could greatly increase the difficulty of an ascent. It is possible that snow in the main or other couloirs could aid in an ascent or offer a glissade; *however*, any glissade down a route which has not been climbed should be done only after careful scouting and with great caution, as a number of steps exist in all of the couloirs.

Piney Lake trailhead to summit: 5 miles
Elevation gain: 4,200 feet
(Route description from September climb)

Mount Powell may also be reached via the Cataract Creek drainage from Highway 9 and Green Mountain Reservoir.

MOUNT RICHTHOFEN
12,940 Feet
Never Summer Range—Front Range

The river that ends in sun-baked mud flats below the international border has its beginnings beneath the rugged ridges of Mount Richthofen. Even below the snowy summits of the Never Summer Range, however, the Colorado River landscape shows evidence of the technology of water-hungry exploiters. The long scar which slants across the eastern slope of the range is the Grand Ditch, the first major project to tap the water wealth of the Colorado River Basin and send it flowing eastward. From these high mountain valleys studded with spruce and fir, the Colorado River begins its journey to the sea, but as Philip Fradkin has sadly described it in a book of the same name, it is already "a river no more."

Things were simpler here in 1879 when Benjamin Franklin Burnett staked out Lulu City, an overnight boom town along the river's meandering banks. Named after Burnett's daughter, Lulu City sprang to life at the clarion call of "Gold!" For a short two years, it thrived, then abruptly dropped into oblivion. By 1883, even the post office was gone. Lulu's memory lingered on a mountain and, for a time, a pass.

Dear Muriel Sibell Wolle tells the story that Lulu City was not so roaring a camp that crime went unpunished. One

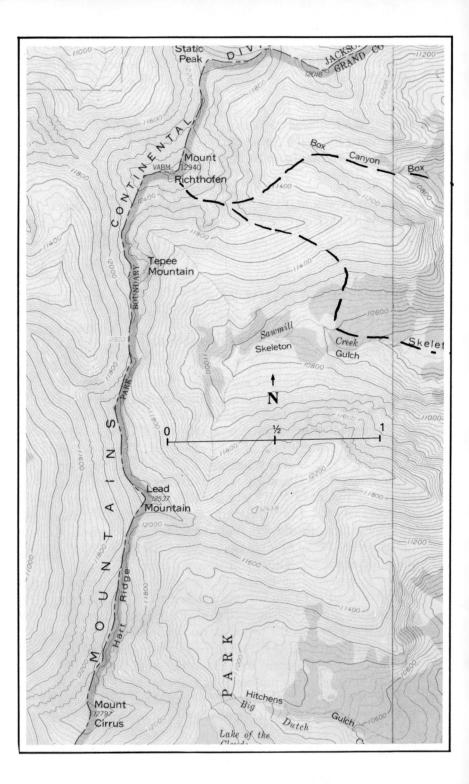

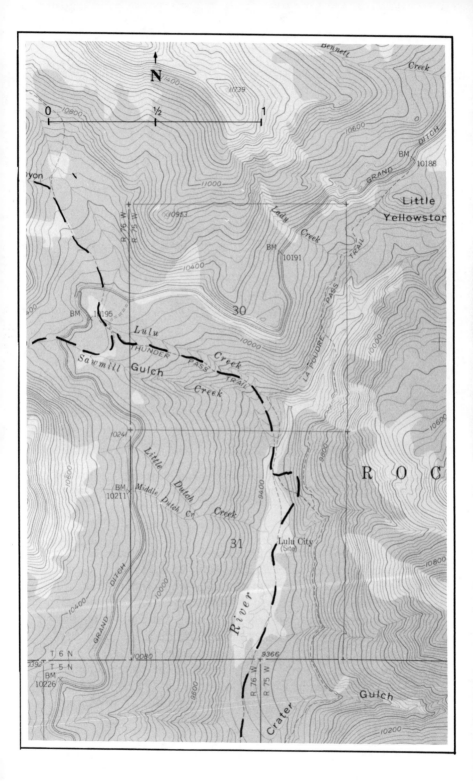

Broad grassy slopes up Richthofen's long southeast ridge rise toward buttress walls. The route goes toward the couloir ("v") above Gary's head.

Saturday night, two German miners, far more than just two sheets to the wind, proceeded to shoot up the town. The local citizenry promptly ran them out. The two Germans struck off up Hitchens Creek toward Mount Cirrus and indignantly founded their own town near timberline. Dutchtown, as they called it, was hardly a threat to Lulu's progress, and it too grew silent when gold and silver's bright promise faded.

Mount Richthofen, the high point of the Never Summer Range, was named by Clarence King for Baron Ferdinand von Richthofen, with whom King had served during the Whitney Survey in California. Baron von Richthofen (not to be confused with his cousin, Baron Walter von Richthofen of Denver's Montclair) developed early theories of volcanic rock and later mapped the mountains of central China. Although Ferdinand was not with King on his surveys of Colorado, King admired his work and named Mount Richthofen after him in 1876, one year before cousin Walter arrived in Denver.

Bill Bueler reports that the first documented ascent of Mount Richthofen was made solo in 1908 by William S. Cooper, a pioneering climber of both the Front and San Juan ranges. It seems probable, however, that if two Germans got fed up enough with Lulu City to start their own town, at least one other soul may have braved Richthofen's summit before the daring Mr. Cooper.

Northeast of Mount Richthofen is Thunder Pass, also known as Lulu Pass, over which a stage road once ran into North Park. East of Thunder Pass is La Poudre Pass, over which the Grand Ditch empties Western Slope water into Long Draw Reservoir. During the heyday of Lulu City, stages from Fort Collins crossed La Poudre Pass three times a week after a journey along the rough Cache La Poudre River.

THE ROUTES
Rocky Mountain National Park
Fall River Pass 7½ Quad
Mount Richthofen 7½ Quad

Skeleton Gulch: From the Grand Lake turnoff, drive north on U.S. 34, into Rocky Mountain National Park to the Phantom Valley trailhead. Hike north on the trail marked "La Poudre Pass Trail, Lulu City, Thunder Pass." The trail runs easily along the Colorado River, through Shipler Park, for three miles to Lulu City, where few vestiges remain of the mining boom of 1879. From Lulu City the trail climbs slightly east and uphill and then descends to cross the Colorado River and head for Thunder Pass. (There are several trail junctions, but they are all adequately marked.)

Stay on the trail bound for Thunder Pass as it climbs steeply northwest along the Lulu Creek drainage. At the west side of

Ditch Camp #3, take the marked trail for Mount Richthofen and Skeleton Gulch—it takes off west, crossing the Grand Ditch and climbing west up Skeleton Gulch. The rugged slopes of Teepee Mountain soon come into view at the head of the gulch, with Mount Richthofen rising further to the north.

Climb Mount Richthofen's long southeast ridge via any number of gullies running down into Skeleton Gulch. The ridge is long and grassy, leading to what at first appears to be a rather difficult buttress at the head of the ridge. To the north (right) the ridge drops steeply into upper Box Canyon. To the left there is a notch high in the head of the main buttress. Pick a route which strikes for a smaller notch topped by a cairn between these two features. From here, the route is obvious along a crumbling trail. Richthofen's rock is extremely loose, and the upper reaches have much crumbling talus and scree.

Approximately 600 feet below the summit is a saddle which is reached shortly after passing through the small notch described above. This saddle can also be reached by continuing northwest up Skeleton Gulch (beneath Teepee Mountain) and then swinging back east (right). This approach lends itself to the adventurous who may wish to attempt Teepee Mountain's awesome-looking twin summits. Mount Richthofen is a great brewer of thunderstorms, and the Never Summer Peaks are appropriately named—ice axes are highly recommended.

From the saddle below Mount Richthofen's summit is a superb couloir which descends east into the Box Canyon drainage. This may be taken as an alternate descent route or as a speedy glissade exit for properly equipped parties, should thunderstorms threaten. The Box Canyon drainage returns one to the Thunder Pass Trail.

Phantom Valley trailhead to summit: 6.5 miles
Elevation gain: 3,900 feet, plus 250 on return.
(Route description from July climb)

PARKVIEW MOUNTAIN
12,296 Feet
Rabbit Ears Range

Parkview Mountain provides just that—stunning views of the broad expanses of North and Middle parks. The mountain is the high point in the thirty-mile-long Rabbit Ears Range, which runs from Rabbit Ears Pass on the west to the Never Summer Range on the east, and which forms the southern boundary of North Park. The Park Range to the northwest and the Rawah Range to the northeast complete North Park's necklace of mountains. The Continental Divide runs the entire length of the Rabbit Ears Range, dividing the headwaters of the North Platte River from those of the Colorado.

The summit of Parkview Mountain is the distant point in the middle background. This view looks west from near Willow Creek Pass. The other route described climbs the left-hand skyline.

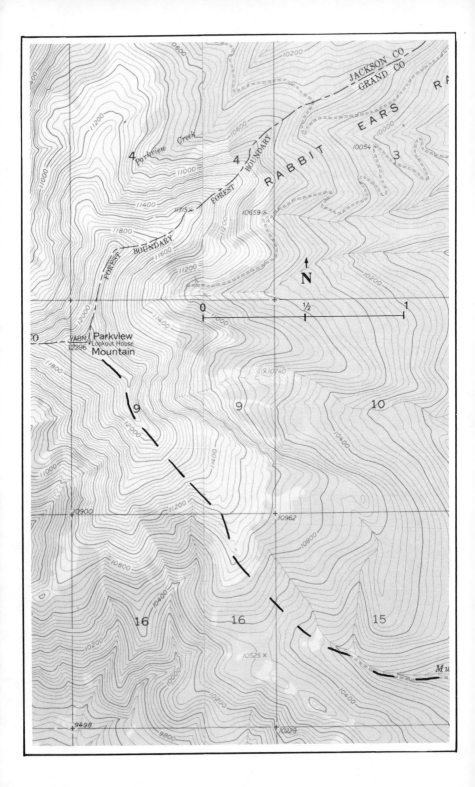

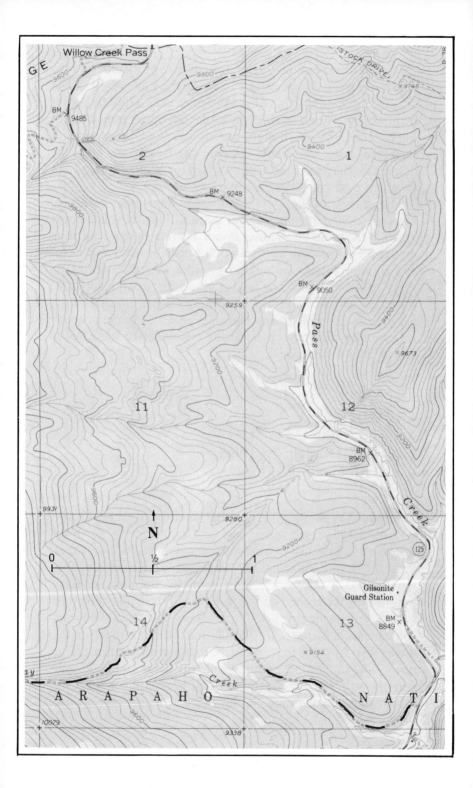

Parkview was climbed and named in 1873 by members of the Hayden Survey. Its seems safe to speculate, however, that Ute or other Indians may have used the summit as a lookout point from which to scout the buffalo herds that once roamed North Park. The Hayden Report noted that "on either side of Parkview Peak the divide between the two parks falls, the descent on the east to the headwaters of the Willow being . . . an excellent pass connecting the parks."

The slopes of Parkview Mountain have seen extensive logging. Downed timber and a maze of logging roads cover much of the mountain's lower slopes. Remnants of an old mine are visible in the basin northeast of the peak beneath the divide, and an abandoned fire lookout presides over the summit.

Aside from the view and the rather quaint lookout, Parkview Mountain's most interesting feature consists of the heavy cornices which hang from the peak's long north-south ridges until midsummer—a strong testament to the force of North Park's winds!

THE ROUTES
Arapaho National Forest
Parkview Mountain 7½ Quad
Radial Mountain 7½ Quad

Willow Creek Pass: From the junction of U.S. 40 and Colorado 125, three miles west of Granby, drive north on Colorado 125 twenty-two miles to the summit of Willow Creek Pass, 9,621 feet. After mile 17, Parkview Mountain is plainly visible to the west. From the summit of the pass, or from pullouts on the several curves just to the south, hike west on a variety of logging trails. You cannot get lost, only inconvenienced, by the maze of trails, but the idea is to follow the divide west from the pass, climb the mountain's northeast ridge just below timberline, and proceed southwest and south one and one-half miles to the summit. The heavy timber along the ridge can hold corn snow on this route well into June, as one tired golden retriever can attest.

Willow Creek Pass to summit: 3 miles
Elevation gain: 2,700 feet
(Route description from June climb)

Mulstay Creek/Parkview Mountain Trail: A longer route, which offers not only cross-country ski possibilities in winter but also jeep access well above timberline in summer, starts from mile 17 on Colorado 125 just south of a road heading east from 125 to Vagabond Ranch. At one time, and perhaps again, this road was marked "Parkview Mountain Trail." A logging road follows the Mulstay Creek drainage west for almost two miles and then forks, with one branch continuing up the drainage and the other turning northwest (right) onto Parkview's broad southeast flank. Take the right-hand fork, which continues climbing moderately for about one-half mile and then swings due north for a straight shot across the flank. After almost one-half mile up this straightaway, a series of red tags marks a side road going west (left). Hike up this fork another mile to timberline, a total of four miles from the highway.

From here the road continues up the mountain's southeast flank. When the road peters out, simply continue upward toward the rocks marking the crest of the long summit plateau. Once on the plateau, the summit is an easy matter of a quarter of a mile and 500 vertical feet to the north. In early season, care should be taken to avoid the cornices which encrust the Parkview ridges.

Colorado 125 to summit: 5 miles
Elevation gain: 3,500 feet
(Route description from July climb)

MOUNT ZIRKEL
12,180 Feet
Park Range

Mount Zirkel is the high point of the Park Range along which the Continental Divide separates the waters of the North Platte River flowing north to Wyoming from the Elk River flowing south to the Yampa River. Lest anyone be deceived by its low elevation, Mount Zirkel is a rough mountain. It is isolated in the heart of the Mount Zirkel Wilderness Area and is a brewer of fickle weather. One of my frequent climbing companions, a veteran of some two hundred ascents, failed to reach the summit in his first three attempts because of the mountain's vagaries.

The Mount Zirkel area is filled with charming lakes and glacial features. The Zirkel-Big Agnes-Sawtooth uplift is comprised of hornblende schist and greenstone, accounting for its rugged appearance within sight of flat-topped mounds. Two passes cross the Park Range just south of Mount Zirkel—Red Dirt Pass, the origin of its name easily understood, and Ute Pass, one of at least five Ute Passes in the state, named because an early Ute trail crossed from North Park to the Steamboat Springs area. West of Mount Zirkel is 10,839-foot Hahns Peak, named after goldseeker Joseph Hahn. Hahns Peak is a highly eroded laccolith, curiously located well west of the range.

Mount Zirkel was named by Clarence King for Ferdinand Zirkel, a German petrologist who in 1874 contributed his expertise to King's Fortieth Parallel Survey. Petrology is the science of the description and classification of rocks, and King and Zirkel spent long hours discussing the relationship between European and American rocks and the associated problems of nomenclature. Zirkel's *Microscopical Petrology* appeared as part of King's report and was largely responsible for American scientists taking the science seriously.

Lack of extensive mining activity nearby and its relatively low elevation deprived Mount Zirkel of early climbing history. According to Bill Bueler, a Forest Service publication as late as

Mount Zirkel looking north from its southwest sub-peak. *Gary R. Koontz photo.*

1917 noted that "its rocky pinnacle has never yet been scaled." Carl Melzer and his party, while on their epic Continental Divide trek of 1936, reached the summit and found no written record, although there was evidence of previous visitors.

THE ROUTES
Routt National Forest
Mount Zirkel 7½ Quad

   Slavonia: From just west of downtown Steamboat Springs, on U.S. 40, drive north on Routt County 129 for 17.3 miles to the town of Clark and another one-half mile to the intersection of Routt County 64, also marked as Forest Service 400.

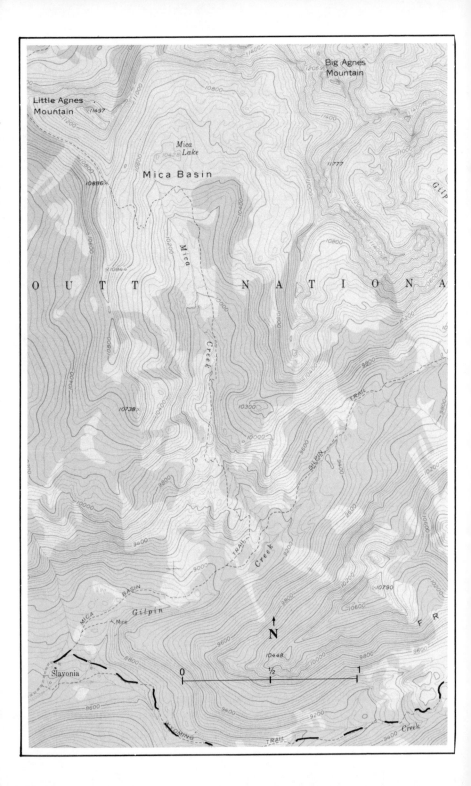

Big Agnes
Mountain

Little Agnes
Mountain

11497

10886

*Mica
Lake*

Mica Basin

11777

Gilpin

10844

O   U   T   T   N   A   T   I   O   N   A

Mica

Creek

10738

10300

10000

10790

10790

MICA   BASIN

Gilpin

Mine

Gilpin

Creek

TRAIL

TRAIL

N

10448

F   R

Slavonia

0   ½   1

WYOMING

TRAIL

Creek

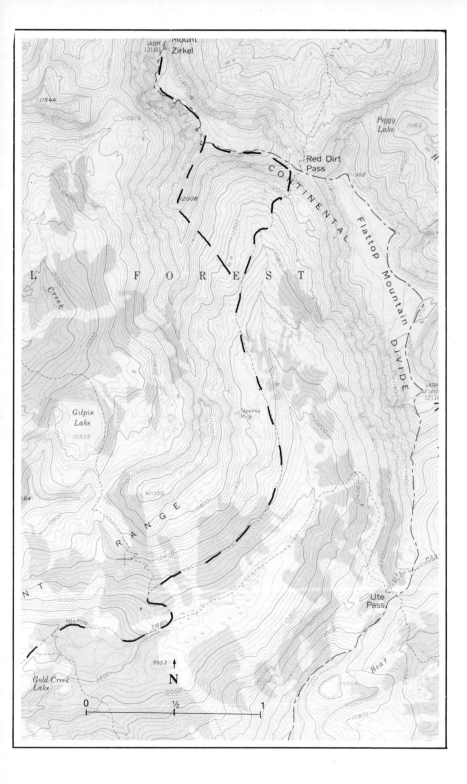

Continue northeast on Routt County 64 for a total of 12.1 miles to Slavonia and the Forest Service trailheads.

The Forest Service has altered some of the trails shown on the Mount Zirkel quad. As of this writing, both the Gilpin Creek Trail and the Gold Creek Trail leave from the same parking area just north of where Gilpin Creek and Gold Creek converge to form the Elk River. Hike north from the trailhead several hundred yards to where the trails split. Hike east on the Gold Creek Trail for two and one-half miles to Gold Creek Lake, which offers a number of fine campsites in the surrounding terrain. From the lake, continue northeast past the Wyoming Trail intersection. Cross Gold Creek and proceed to an intersection one mile from the lake where the trail emerges from a narrow valley into a large marshy meadow. A short distance north (uphill) of this point the trail splits again with the north (left) branch continuing over the ridge to Gilpin Lake and the east (right) branch contouring first northeast and then north a total of three miles to Red Dirt Pass.

From Red Dirt Pass, climb northwest for one mile along a flat ridge to Mount Zirkel's summit. Depending on snow conditions, climbers may wish to leave the trail short of Red Dirt Pass and climb northwest to a 12,006-foot point and then follow the ridge northeast a short distance to this same flat ridge. While Mount Zirkel's south ridge presents no technical challenges, there are impressive dropoffs, particularly to the west—the ridge involves a number of minor ups and downs. This 12,006-foot point may also be reached by taking the Gilpin Trail fork just beyond the trailhead and climbing northeast from Gilpin Lake.

Trailhead to summit via Red Dirt Pass: 7.5 miles
Elevation gain: 3,700 feet
(Route description from October climb)

Part 2
Sawatch and
Sangre De Cristo Ranges

The broad-ridged monarchs of the Sawatch Range are well-deserving of their frequent sobriquet "Backbone of a Continent." The broad-ridged character of the range does not stop at the fifteen Sawatch Fourteeners, however, but extends to such superb thirteeners as Grizzly, Hope, Casco, and French. Ice Mountain, challenging from any side, is a spectacular exception. While the San Luis Valley keeps the Sangre de Cristo Range well east of the Continental Divide, it is included in this section because in file like sentinels its peaks continue to give the impression of a backbone running south toward New Mexico.

The peaks in this part of the guide include moderate beginner or family climbs such as Mount Aetna and Taylor Mountain, both within easy reach of U.S. 50. Intriguing historical sites and superb views abound on the slopes of Mount Ouray above Marshall Pass, and from Grizzly Peak above colorful mining camps. Mountaineering challenges can be found on Ice Mountain and Mount Adams, an overlooked but deserving neighbor of the Crestones.

Beyond this sampling, there are other grand possibilities. The areas around Grizzly Peak and west of Mount Massive offer many overlooked climbs, including the illusive Mount Oklahoma. And, while Fourteener-baggers run rampant over much of the Sawatch Range, the Sangre de Cristo Peaks offer great backpacking and climbing combinations, particularly along the Rainbow Trail or south of the Crestones along the Huerfano River drainages. Finally, a favorite still on my list is stately Mount Antora at the tail end of the Sawatch.

GRIZZLY PEAK
13,988 Feet
Sawatch Range

Sitting squarely on the Continental Divide six miles south of Independence Pass, Grizzly Peak is far more than just a member of the "Once a Fourteener Club." Formerly measured at an even 14,000 feet, Grizzly was resurveyed in 1965 and assigned its present height. Interestingly enough, had Grizzly continued to be included in the ranks of Fourteeners, this would have made it one of only three Fourteeners to sit squarely on the Continental Divide (joining Grays and Torreys) and one of only three Fourteeners named for animals (joining Little Bear and Culebra—Spanish for "snake"). While the name "Grizzly" abounds on lesser summits, the indomitable Bob Ormes appropriately suggests the nomenclature of "Grizzly Major" for this fine mountain.

Grizzly Peak looking south up the Lincoln Creek drainage.

"Name that Fourteener!" The summit block of Grizzly Peak.

Grizzly, like its neighboring Fourteener La Plata Peak, was probably first climbed by miners in search of silver. The earliest recorded ascent of each was by a Hayden Survey party during the summer of 1873. Reportedly, team members observed a grizzly bear floating on an ice floe in one of the lakes at the base of the peak. Certainly, grizzlies were no strangers to the early surveys and seem to have made a number of first ascents on their own!

Grizzly Peak lies in the heart of the Red Mountain Mining District. In the 1890s, the town of Ruby was laid out southwest of the mountain in the basin at the head of the Lincoln Creek drainage. Mines were located on both sides of the Divide, and claim markers still dot the ridge crest between Grizzly and Garfield peaks. Most mines, including the once promising Ruby and Galena Belle, produced ruby silver with scatterings

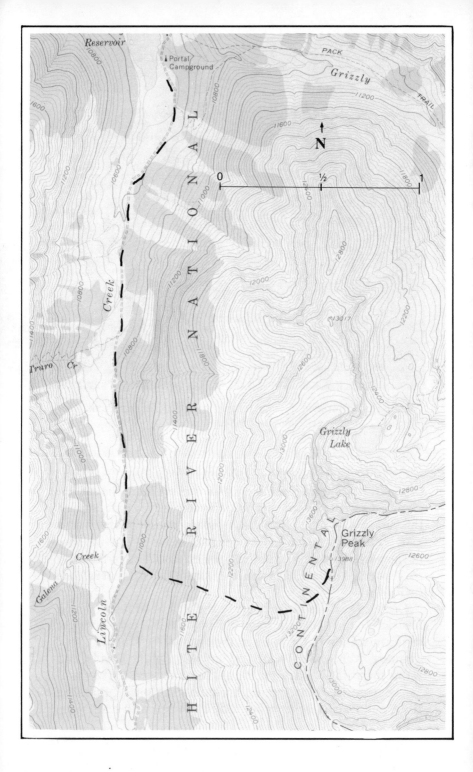

of gold, lead, iron, and molybdenum. In time, the lack of adequate transportation and declining silver prices pushed Ruby into ruin.

THE ROUTES
White River National Forest
Independence Pass 7½ Quad

Grizzly Reservoir: From ten miles west of the summit of Independence Pass on Colorado 82, turn south and follow the Lincoln Creek access road seven miles to Grizzly Reservoir and Portal Campground. The road is generally passable to passenger cars as far as the campground. The road above the reservoir continues on another four miles to the ghost town of Ruby and is passable in jeeps, four-wheel drives, and those Volkswagons thinking themselves jeeps.

From Portal Campground, hike south on the road for two and one-half miles to the base of a broad gully descending from the saddle just south (right) of the summit. An earlier couloir, easily recognizable from the "fang" guarding the northern side is better avoided as steeper and more rotten. Ascend the gully to the saddle, a distance of one mile, and then continue a short distance north along the ridge to the summit. This is an interesting point in that there are two rather rugged blocks of almost equal height separated by a thirty-foot drop—and with some spectacular dropoffs to the east. The blocks are not difficult, but you should exercise caution if snow or wet conditions exist.

From Grizzly Peak, an interesting side trip is to hike one mile south along the Continental Divide to 13,760-foot Garfield Peak, which offers impressive views of both Grizzly and a colonnaded peak just to the east. Stay to the west (right) on the Grizzly-Garfield ridge, skirting a small point. Depending on the side trip to Garfield, descend either the main gully from the Grizzly saddle or a sandy couloir dropping west of the saddle between the small point and Garfield Peak. The rock here is loose with some sand and small scree. At least one guidebook author, who shall of course remain anonymous,

Grizzly Peak looking north from the summit of Garfield Peak.

suffered a badly sprained ankle when loose sand in one steep couloir camouflaged the icy remnants of the previous winter. No record remains of his remarks!

Portal Campground to summit: 3½ miles
Elevation gain: 3,400 feet

Total trip with Garfield: 9 miles
Elevation gain: 3,800 feet

(Route description from August climb)

While the route described above is an intermediate climb in favorable conditions, a number of other more adventurous routes on Grizzly Peak rise from Grizzly Lake, Graham Gulch, and McNasser Gulch. All seem to require a difficult ascent of the mountain's east ridge, which combines several broken sections with a sharp dropoff on the Grizzly Lake (north) side.

7-3-2000

CASCO PEAK
13,908 Feet
Sawatch Range

7-3-2000

FRENCH MOUNTAIN
13,922 Feet
Sawatch Range

The twin summits of Casco Peak and French Mountain stand above the basin of South Halfmoon Creek. Though obscured from most eyes by the mass of Mount Elbert, each summit easily qualifies for inclusion on the list of the one hundred highest peaks in Colorado.

In 1874, Hayden Survey members made the first recorded ascent of Casco and French's famous neighbor to the east. First ascent records are in doubt for Casco and French, but wandering prospectors are odds on favorites for the honor. Equally in doubt are the origins of the names, although again

Looking north from the summit of Casco Peak to infamous Frasco (left) and French Mountain (right). Mount Massive sprawls in the background.

they probably came from prospectors or mines or, in the case of French, perhaps the nationality of some individual. Mining activity surrounded the peaks and included such claims as the Champion to the west, the Iron Mike in the basin between the peaks, and the Last Chance and Golden Fleece in Echo Basin to the south.

Casco and French are joined by a broken ridge which features a sharp point near the Casco-French saddle and to the north, a 13,876-foot high point labeled "Frasco" by the U.S. Geological Survey. Views from the summits of both peaks feature the giants of Mounts Elbert, Massive, and La Plata and a particularly fine vista of the frequently overlooked summits west of Mount Massive, including 13,845-foot Mount Oklahoma.

Looking south from the summit of French Mountain to Bull Hill (foreground left) and La Plata Peak (background right).

THE ROUTES
San Isabel National Forest
Mount Elbert 7½ Quad
Mount Massive 7½ Quad

South Halfmoon Creek: From the trailer park at Malta, three miles west of Leadville on U.S. 24, drive west eight-tenths of a mile on Colorado 300. Turn left and proceed south on Lake County 11, bearing right at mile 1.2 where the road forks, and continue another 4 miles to Halfmoon Campground. Continue west for approximately 3.3 miles to another fork, and there turn south (left), immediately crossing a rickety bridge over Halfmoon Creek. Camping is available near the

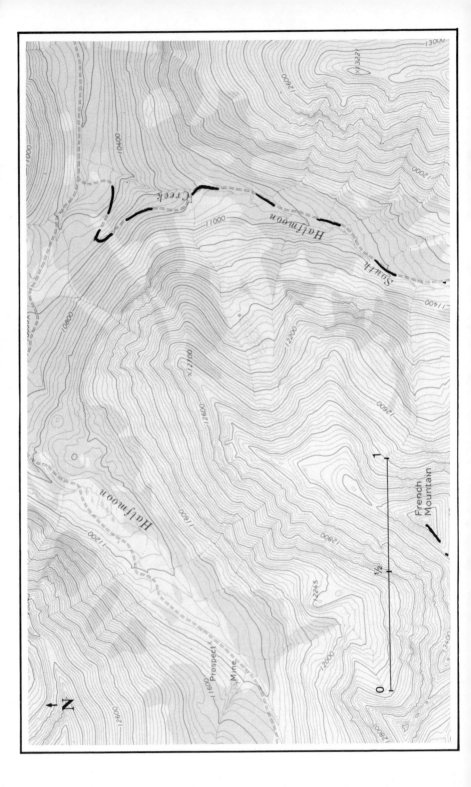

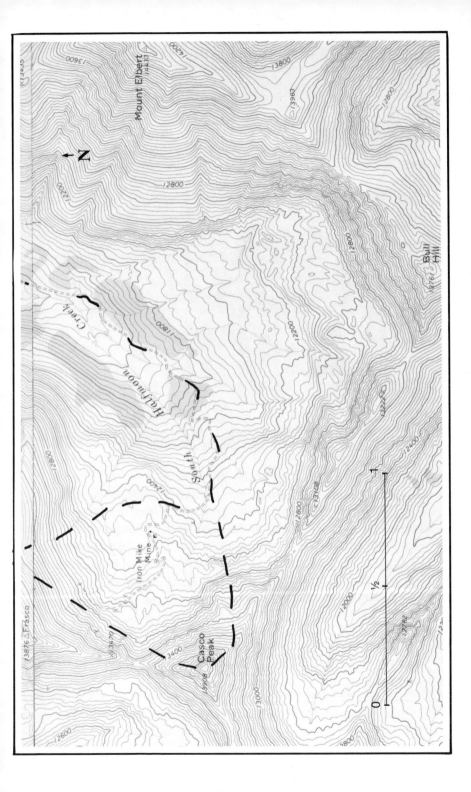

"What? No glissade?" Casco Peak from the northeast after a descent of French Mountain.

bridge or at a number of locations between there and the campground. Generally, the road is passable in cars as far as this bridge after mid-June.

Hike south across the bridge and up a mining road into the basin of South Halfmoon Creek. After three miles, the old mining road turns sharply to the west and then climbs to the Iron Mike Mine in the basin between Casco Peak to the south and French Mountain to the north. Leave the road where it swings north and climb southwest up a combination of grassy slopes and some talus to the southeast ridge of Casco. It is an easy scramble northwest to Casco's summit, which is a collection of large boulders.

Descend Casco Peak on the north side, working your way down the ridge and several small scree couloirs. Drop below the Casco-French saddle and contour toward the low point just below the main southwest ridge of French Mountain. Dropping down a thousand feet may seem frustrating, but this is the most expedient and direct route to French Mountain.

(You could mount the ridge south of Frasco and continue north to French, climbing Frasco en route, but there is no real reason to do so, unless you are particularly infatuated with Frasco. Two intrepid climbers once did this latter route only to reach the summit of Frasco and find that their female companion, with whom they had left the summit of Casco and who had dropped below for the direct route, was waving to them from the summit of French. Nice going, Dolora!)

There is a fine, long shoestring couloir which leads from the Frasco-French saddle back to near the Iron Mike Mine road. In early season, this should be a superb glissade route back to the road. It is also possible to drop northeast off French, but this route has much scree and talus late in the season.

Trailhead to Casco: 4.5 miles
Elevation gain: 3,700 feet

Casco to French direct: 1.2 miles
Elevation gain: about 1,000 feet

Casco to French via Frasco: 1.5 miles
Elevation gain: about 1,300 feet

Total climb with Casco to French direct: 10 miles
Elevation gain: 4,700 feet

(Route description from July climb)

ICE MOUNTAIN
13,951 Feet
Sawatch Range

Ice Mountain and its sister summits, which join to form the Three Apostles, rise in dramatic contrast to the surrounding peaks of the Sawatch Range. From the rounded ridges and summits of the surrounding Sawatch, the ruggedness of the Three Apostles is a spectacular sight. Once thought to be a

Ice Mountain looking north from Waterloo Gulch. The North Apostle is to the right, and the summit lies out of sight beyond the point just right of the shoestring couloir. *Gary R. Koontz photo.*

Fourteener, Ice Mountain is certainly worthy of inclusion on the list and much more challenging than most.

The first known ascent of Ice Mountain came late. The Wheeler and Hayden surveys avoided the tough terrain as well as the rounded summits of Missouri, Belford, and Oxford peaks running off to the east. Miners scoured the upper basin of the South Fork of Clear Creek and Harrison Flat for silver, and for a time developed the tiny settlement of Hamilton, but there is no documented evidence of an Ice Mountain ascent until John L.J. Hart's climb of October 4, 1931. The late date of that climb and a report of it by Josiah G. Holland, Hart's partner in both law and mountaineering, supports Ice Mountain's tough reputation.

Holland's report of the first ascent makes interesting reading in the November 1931 issue of *Trail and Timberline*. Holland, Hart, Ted Hanington, and Erl Ellis left Denver on October 3, expecting a pleasant fall climb. "For this reason," wrote Holland, "the equipment carried by three of us consisted of tennis shoes and light clothes, while the Editor [Hart], conforming to old climbing habits, took proper nailed boots and a ski cap."

Initially, the party made a mistake repeated by a later day climbing guide author—they followed a prospect trail well up the west side of Huron Peak before striking over several ridges straight for the mountain. Despite the fact that 1931 had seen an incredibly dry summer (Holland noted that Clear Creek Reservoir was dry), the party found ample snow on the upper

Ice Mountain looking north on the approach to the shoestring couloir. *Gary R. Koontz photo.*

Ice axes were essential for this 4th of July climb up Ice Mountain.
Gary R. Koontz photo.

Even the most conscientious of guidebook authors occasionally comes under criticism. Tim Duffy about to give the author a closer view of the east face. Ice Mountain summit. *Gary R. Koontz photo.*

reaches of the peak. About four hundred feet below the summit, it became obvious that only Hart was properly equipped to continue because, said Holland, "it involved a nearly perpendicular climb of several hundred feet covered with ice and snow—conditions not at all adapted to tennis shoes." Hart continued on alone and reached the summit in a gentle snowstorm. Finding no evidence of an earlier ascent, he built a small cairn, entered a summit record, and returned to his cold companions waiting patiently below.

The first winter ascent of Ice Mountain may have occurred two days late for "official" winter in March of 1976, when a party consisting of Craig Koontz, Gary Kocsis, and Tom Griffiths of Gunnison made a three-day ascent from the Texas Creek drainage.

THE ROUTES
San Isabel National Forest
Gunnison National Forest
Winfield 7½ Quad (New)
Tincup 7½ Quad (New)

Ice Mountain has no easy side and should be approached only by experienced parties.

Waterloo Gulch-Texas Creek drainage: From Taylor Dam, northeast of Gunnison, drive 2.8 miles east and north to the cluster of buildings on the east side of Taylor Reservoir. Turn left at the junction and continue north around the reservoir past the turnoff to Cottonwood Pass, three miles to the Texas Creek road heading east. The turnoff is a bend beyond where Texas Creek flows into the reservoir.

Drive east for nine miles up the Texas Creek drainage on what rapidly becomes four-wheel drive terrain, past the Texas Lakes to the road's end. (About one-half mile from the road's end, keep left where the road forks.) From the road's end, the Timberline Trail leads west toward Prospector Gulch while the Texas Creek Trail continues northeast up the main drainage. After approximately one-half mile, the Timberline Trail forks

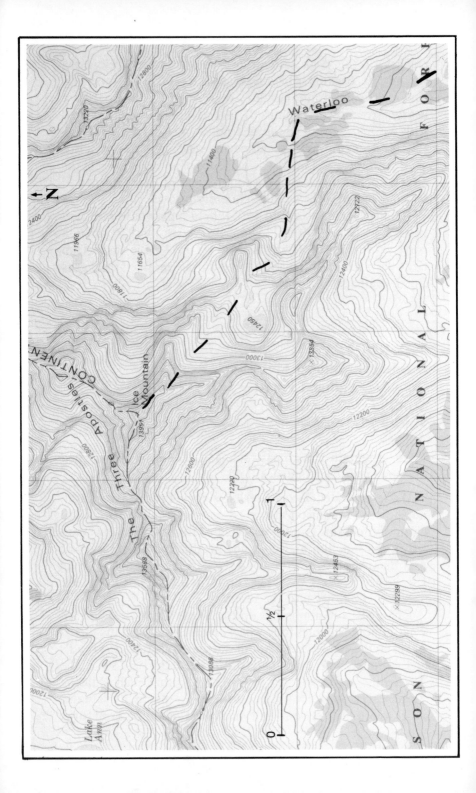

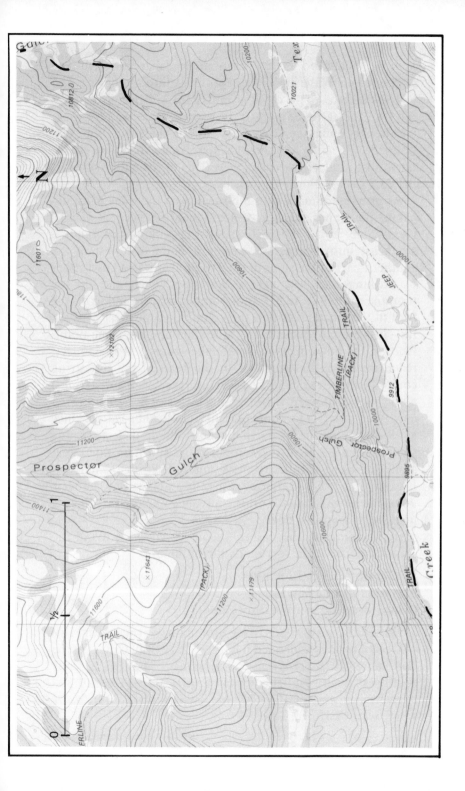

and the Waterloo Gulch Trail angles sharply north and continues up Waterloo Gulch two miles into the basin.

The trail crosses the creek several times, and in high water an old trail and series of game trails seem to work well for those wishing to remain on the west side of the main Waterloo drainage. The first mountain which comes into view at the northwest head of the basin, west (left) of the main saddle, is the 13,863-foot North Apostle.

As progress is made into the basin, past the ruins of an old cabin, the upper reaches of Ice Mountain become visible, identifiable by a narrow shoestring couloir descending southeast into a large bowl from a point just west of the southern part of the summit ridge. Climb into this bowl either by striking due west across Waterloo Gulch and up the moraine south of a 12,520-foot point or by continuing on the trail to the basin lakes and then climbing southwest between the cliffs directly beneath Ice Mountain and the same point. Once in the bowl, where a small lake sparkles at 12,450 feet, reach the notch in the ridge, at the head of the shoestring couloir, either by angling west (left) and then back north (right) along a series of steep, downsloping ledges or by ascending the narrow couloir. Either route presents significant hazards. Once at the notch, climb north several hundred feet to the southeastern point of the summit ridge and then northwest along the ridge .2 miles to the summit. The ridge is narrow, broken, and exposed, but of generally stable rock. The view down the north face will confirm anyone's opinion that there is no easy way up this one!

If glissading on the descent, scout carefully to avoid the series of cliffs which surrounds the mountain.

Trailhead to summit: 5 miles
Elevation gain: 4,000 feet
(Route description from July climb)

The northern approach to Ice Mountain, via the South Fork of Clear Creek, is addressed in Ormes and by Bill Graves in the November 1975 *Trail and Timberline*. The route leads southwest from Winfield, which is on Chaffee County 390 twelve miles west of U.S. 24, and then climbs south up the valley west of Huron Peak.

6-30-2000

MOUNT HOPE
13,933 Feet
Sawatch Range

6-30-2000 QUAIL MOUNTAIN 13.461 Feet

Mount Hope is the dominant peak as you look southwest across the waters of Twin Lakes. Its rather flat and roomy summit is a sharp contrast to the mountain's rugged appearance from almost every direction. To the east is the 13,461-foot summit of Quail Mountain, while to the west is La Plata Peak with its jagged buzzsaw, Ellingwood Ridge. Between Mount Hope and La Plata Peak is an unnamed mountain, 13,783 feet high, which comes close to inclusion in the one hundred highest in Colorado. A trail via Sheep and

Cloud-shrouded Mount Hope, looking southwest from just north of the Twin Lakes turnoff. The approach from the south hits the saddle between Quail Mountain (left) and Mount Hope, climbing west up the east ridge to the rounded summit.

Along Mount Hope's east ridge on a cloudy, misty morning. *Gary R. Koontz photo.*

Little Willis gulches crosses the 12,500-foot saddle between Mount Hope and Quail Mountain, a saddle that connects the drainages of Clear Creek and Lake Creek.

The mining industry trod heavily in this vicinity, and the summits of Mount Hope and Quail Mountain were probably reached first by prospectors in search of silver. The rush to Aspen in the early 1880s found the Lake Creek road to the north filled with wagons and pack trains bound for Independence Pass, while to the south the towns of Vicksburg, Rockdale, and Winfield boomed for a time along Clear Creek.

THE ROUTES
San Isabel National Forest
Winfield 7½ Quad
Mount Elbert 7½ Quad

Sheep Gulch-East Ridge: From two miles south of Granite, between Buena Vista and Leadville on U.S. 24, drive west on

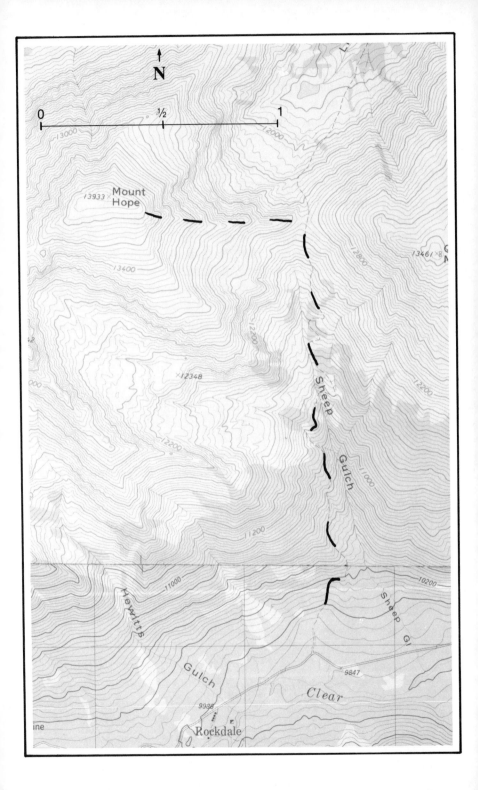

N

0   ½   1

13000

12000

Mount
Hope
13933

1346/

12800

13400

1200

12200

×12348

Sheep

12200

12200

1000

Gulch

11200

11000

10200

Hewitts

Sheep Gl

Gulch

9847

Clear

9938

ine

Rockdale

Chaffee County 390 for eight miles to Vicksburg. Continue west an additional 1.6 miles to several small lakes on the south side of the road. A narrow, rutted path leads north from here angling northeast into Sheep Gulch. The road quickly becomes a narrow trail which climbs steeply for two miles through heavy aspen to the saddle between Mount Hope to the west and Quail Mountain to the east. From the saddle, climb west (left) .8 miles up the east ridge of Mount Hope. Although the ridge is narrow with particularly spectacular dropoffs to the north, it is generally a moderate scramble with several steep sections. Hope's summit offers fine views of the Clear Creek Valley Fourteeners to the south, La Plata peak to the west, and Mounts Elbert and Massive to the north.

Descend via the east ridge, or drop southeast across the broad summit plateau and hike down the basin running east beneath the east ridge. In the early season, this route can offer a fine glissade. (Take care, particularly in poor visibility, to avoid descending the gully which drops directly south from the summit, unless you are willing to put up with the rigors of a large talus slope at its base.) The continuation of the summit plateau runs southeast and forms the ridge which is the southwestern boundary of the basin beneath the east ridge. Ormes recommends this route or some combination of it through the basin for the climb, but the east ridge proper is definitely worth the challenge for experienced parties. The saddle between Mount Hope and Quail Mountain can also be reached from the Twin Lakes drainage via Little Willis Gulch.

Sheep Gulch trailhead to summit: 2.8 miles
Elevation gain: 4,100 feet
(Route description from June climb)

6-1-2002

MOUNT AETNA
13,745 Feet
Sawatch Range

6-1-2002

TAYLOR MOUNTAIN
13,651 Feet
Sawatch Range

Mount Aetna and Taylor Mountain are the high points of the ridge which separates the North and Middle forks of the South Arkansas River near Monarch Pass. The peaks are particularly prominent looking north from the summit of the pass, and their proximity to U.S. 50, coupled with the superb glissade potential, make them good winter or early season climbs.

Mining activity was extensive throughout the southern Sawatch Range and miners probably made the first ascents of both summits. Diggings and corner posts are evident quite near the summit of Taylor Mountain. The name "Aetna" seems to have been bestowed in reference to the famous Mount Aetna (or Etna) in Sicily, an active volcano known for its frequent and destructive eruptions. For the record, "Etna" was, in Greek mythology, the mass of rock under which Zeus buried the fire-breathing monster Typhon. (Try that bit of trivia on a climbing companion!) Of course, the rock continued to smoke and burn. Taylor has a more earthly origin and was probably named for a prospector or neighboring mine.

The rush of the early 1880s saw the mining camp of Clifton, soon to be called Shavano, spring up to the north of Aetna and Taylor peaks. The town itself was short-lived, but sporadic mining activity has continued along the North Fork.

To the south, Junction City was established in 1880 where the Middle Fork joins the main stem of the South Arkansas River. Named because the trail forked to climb Chalk Creek Pass to the northwest and Monarch Pass to the south, Junction City was re-christened Garfield in 1883 by the U.S. Postal

Mount Aetna (left) and Taylor Mountain (right) from Monarch Pass.

Department to honor the assassinated President James A. Garfield. A number of rich mines, including the Columbus at the head of Columbus Gulch and the Lily in Taylor Gulch, gave the town some economic stability. A stamp mill on the banks of the Middle Fork handled ore carried from the Columbus Mine by a bucket tramway, the vestiges of which can still be seen.

When the silver mines faltered, Garfield withered, but it hung on as a stop on the highway across Monarch Pass, which became an all-weather route in 1939. Garfield today bears little resemblance to a mining camp, although a large limestone quarry remains in operation nearby. The town now exists on traffic from the Monarch Ski Area and snowbound travelers from Monarch Pass.

THE ROUTES
San Isabel National Forest
Garfield, Colorado 7½ Quad (New)

Southern Approaches: From just west of the Highway Department buildings at Garfield, Chaffee County Road 230 runs northwest up the Middle Fork of the South Arkansas. While this dirt road is passable to four-wheel drives during the summer, I recommend Aetna and Taylor as early season climbs—park in the wide area at the U.S. 50 intersection.

Mount Aetna from Monarch Pass, featuring the grand couloir and the traverse east (right) toward Taylor Mountain.

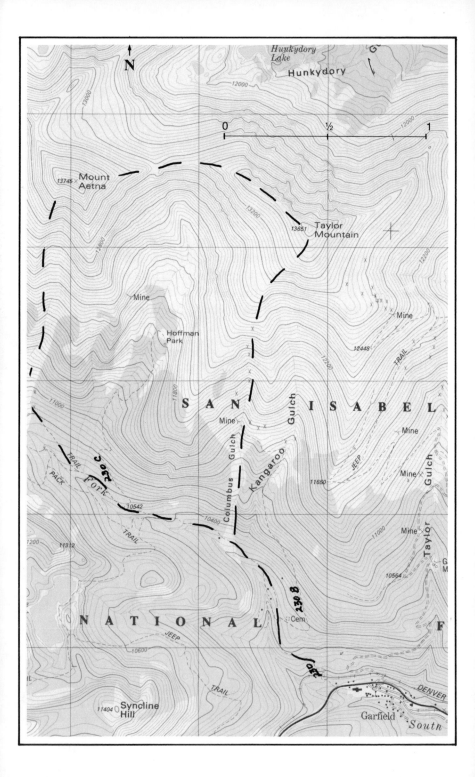

Looking north up Columbus Gulch toward Taylor Mountain.

Hike generally northwest up County Road 230, quickly crossing the tracks of the Denver and Rio Grande's Monarch Branch and continuing one mile to the ruins of the old Columbus Gulch stamp mill. From there, climb north through the aspens up Columbus Gulch along the remains of the Columbus Mine tramway to the mine itself at 11,400 feet. The mine can also be reached via a road which leaves County Road 230 approximately halfway between U.S. 50 and the stamp mill ruins. Continue to the head of Columbus Gulch or, if snow conditions warrant, angle toward the skyline, and follow the ridge/shoulder combination northeast to the summit.

For the traverse to Mount Aetna, continue northwest along the long summit ridge of Taylor Mountain, staying just below the crest on the south (left) side. At the 13,000-foot low point of the 1.2-mile ridge, a short, steep section leads to Mount Aetna's rocky but generally stable east ridge. Once on the summit, if experience and season permit, the classic descent is a 2,500-foot glissade down Aetna's "Great Couloir." Care must be taken to avoid cornices on the west lip of the couloir, and snow conditions may require dropping some distance down the west lip before entering the couloir. From the foot of the couloir, County Road 230 runs southeast two miles back to U.S. 50.

Highway 50 to Taylor summit: 2.6 miles
Elevation gain: 4,000 feet

With traverse to Aetna, round trip: 6.3 miles
Elevation gain: 4,750 feet

(Route description from early June climb)

7-19-2000

MOUNT OURAY
13,971 Feet
Sawatch Range

While learning to fly some years ago in Gunnison, I impressed my instructor with my navigational proficiency. He assumed it was from a knowledgeable reliance on the instrument panel. Actually, it was because the solitary presence of Mount Ouray was always a towering landmark. Indeed, while its prominence is frequently obscured from the depths of the surrounding valleys, from the air Mount Ouray truly deserves the geographic designation "peak." Only 13,266-foot Mount Antora seven miles to the south and 12,853-foot Chipeta Peak several miles to the north attempt to intrude into Mount Ouray's commanding presence. On a clear day, a 360-degree panorama of more than one hundred miles spreads out from its summit.

Mount Ouray takes its name from the famed Ute chieftain. The grand cirque which dominates the mountain's east face and the ridges which come off its summit to the northeast and

Snow accents Mount Ouray's prominence and clearly marks its west ridge descending to the Continental Divide. Marshall Pass is the low point to the south (right). *Aerial photo by Dow Helmers.*

southeast resemble a huge chair. Here, legend has it, the spirit of Chief Ouray sits, ever watchful to what occurs below.

Even before Ouray's time, however, the mountain gazed down upon important events. In 1779, Juan Bautista de Anza, the Spanish governor of New Mexico, marched north up the San Luis Valley and across Poncha Pass beneath the mountain on what became the first documented European penetration of the inner Colorado Rockies.

Almost a century later, in November of 1873, William Marshall, a young army lieutenant with the Wheeler Survey,

111

Mount Ouray and the Chief's prominent "chair" guard the Marshall Pass route running west across the Peak's south shoulder. Sharp eyes will note Uncompahgre Peak rising in the distance above the summit of the pass. *Aerial photo by Dow Helmers.*

stumbled across the 10,846-foot pass on the mountain's southwest slope. Marshall Pass soon became the route of an Otto Mears toll road which boasted of being the "shortest and most direct route to the Gunnison country and all points in the San Juans." Time moved fast, however, and for a tidy $13,000 Mears quickly sold his road to a scrappy outfit bent on building a railroad empire.

In the spring of 1881, William Jackson Palmer's Denver and Rio Grande Railway attacked the slopes of Mount Ouray and Marshall Pass in force in a race to beat the Denver South Park and Pacific Railroad to the prize of the Gunnison country. From Mears Junction, on present-day U.S. 285, the line snaked its narrow gauge rails west up Poncha Creek through the long-since-deserted tank towns of Shirley, Keene, Grays Siding, and Pocono to reach the remarkably level summit of Marshall Pass. Here, at the height of its empire, the Rio Grande had a water tank, coal bin, section house, double-tracked snowshed, turntable, lookout tower, and post office. At the summit, the line crossed the Continental Divide into the Gunnison country and descended sixteen miles of curving four percent grade into Sargents.

When the rails of the Rio Grande were spiked down across Main Street in Gunnison on August 6, 1881, it was not only a victory over the South Park, but most important the inauguration of almost three-quarters of a century of service over Marshall Pass, an enviable record of mountain railroading. In the 1880s, Marshall Pass was the cornerstone of the only transcontinental line through Colorado and of a railroad empire which tied together the vastness of a rugged state and made the ores of Western Slope mines available to the rest of the nation. In that era, the full force of Colorado's commerce and the men responsible for it passed beneath Mount Ouray.

As standard gauge lines diminished the importance of Marshall Pass after the turn of the century, the Rio Grande line retained a close identification with the communities it served. In the 1930s, it was hard to find a classier daycoach than "The Shawano," which operated daily between Salida and Montrose. Then, by a twist of politics, Marshall Pass lost a heated battle to Monarch Pass as the route for U.S. 50, and the new truck traffic that rolled across Monarch soon struck the railroad's death knell. In 1955, the line was abandoned and the roadbed reverted to Gunnison and Saguache counties as an auto road.

Mount Ouray has seen other developments besides the railroad. A ditch dug high on its western slope in the 1880s is one of the earliest instances of transmountain diversion. Water

113

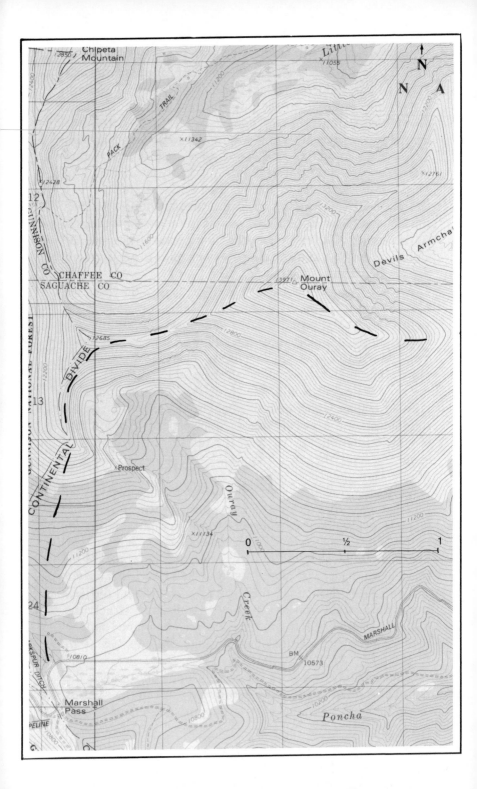

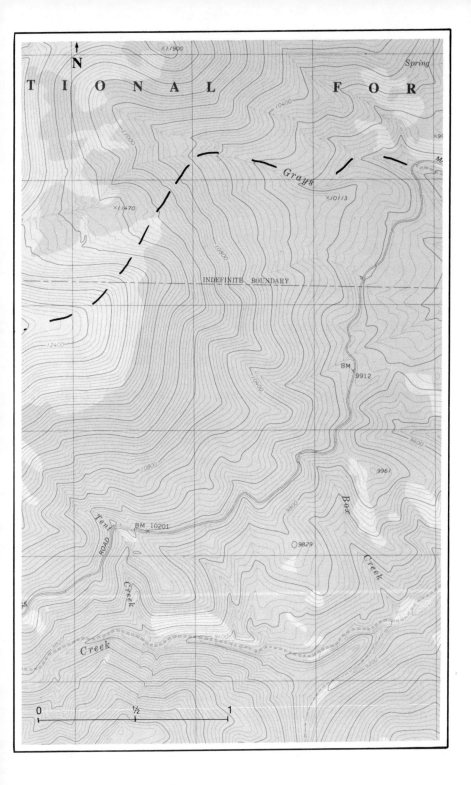

gathered on the western slope of Mount Ouray is channeled across Marshall Pass destined for the Arkansas River and use in Pueblo by the C.F. & I. Steel Corporation. Farther down the western flank of Mount Ouray, the uranium fever of the 1950s struck at the Pinnacle Mine. Now, the site has been taken over by Homestake Mining and is presently a gigantic open pit operation. Trucks laden with ore rumble into Sargents alongside the cinder-littered roadbed of another boom.

THE ROUTES
San Isabel National Forest
Mount Ouray 7½ Quad

Marshall Pass: Drive first to the summit of Marshall Pass via the abandoned Denver and Rio Grande roadbed. From the west, leave Sargents at the foot of Monarch Pass on U.S. 50 and continue east for sixteen miles. (Seven miles above Sargents, the ruins of Tank Seven are visible along Marshall Creek just before the county road and railroad grade become one.) From the east, leave U.S. 285 at Mears Junction six miles south of Poncha Springs. Here, the Rio Grande line splits, one branch going south over Poncha Pass into the San Luis Valley and the other west some fourteen miles to Marshall Pass. The Forest Service campground at O'Haver Lake, west of Mears Junction, makes an ideal campsite.

From the summit of Marshall Pass, Mount Ouray dominates the view to the northeast. There are no questions of "which one is it?" on this climb! During the railroad's glory years, the summit of Marshall Pass was frequently crowded with summer sightseers, many of whom braved the rocky slopes above the station house to climb Mount Ouray.

From the pass, hike north along the eastern crest of the Continental Divide, angling toward the prominent ridge that runs down almost directly west from Ouray's summit. Hitting the tail of the ridge makes for a comparatively gentle climb and avoids a series of bogs and a small cirque on the south slope of the west ridge. Once the ridge narrows and begins to climb, it presents several sections of scrambling among generally larger and stable talus. This gives way to smaller talus the last five hundred feet to the summit.

As promised, the summit view is spectacular, a great place from which to count Fourteeners! Everything from Sneffels to Pikes and Blanca to Snowmass is fair game. Ouray's solitary stance, however, makes it a lightning rod, and afternoon thunderstorms may "spark" one's interest in descending promptly. Early in the season, the southern face may offer some glissade possibilities. Late in the season, the southern slopes are time-consuming talus and poor scree which, when coupled with the bogs at the bottom of the slope, may argue for a descent down the west ridge.

Marshall Pass to summit: 3 miles
Elevation gain: 3,125 feet
(Route description from October climb)

Grays Siding-Southeast Shoulder: A longer climb begins from the old water stop of Grays Siding, six miles east of the Marshall Pass summit. If you camp at O'Haver Lake, hike west from the lake along Grays Creek for about one mile until you reach the main road. This is the old roadbed which is visible looping its way around the lake some 300 feet higher. Cross the main road and continue west up Grays Creek through aspen and some downed timber into the "seat" of Ouray's chair, the basin of the east face cirque. Angle left (south) onto the broad southeast shoulder and continue northwest to the summit. A trail of sorts can usually be found once atop the shoulder.

Grays Siding to summit: 3½ miles
Elevation gain: 4,300 feet
(Route description from July climb)

With appropriate car transportation along the roadbed, you may wish to climb from Grays Siding and then descend the west ridge to the waiting pullman at Marshall Pass. The Marshall Pass is accessible to passenger cars once the spring muds have dried up.

MOUNT ADAMS

UNNAMED 13,546   UNNAMED 13,580 £

13,931 Feet
Sangre de Cristo Range

Mount Adams lies in the heart of the Sangre de Cristo Range just to the north of Kit Carson Peak and the rugged Crestones. Between Mount Adams and Kit Carson Peak is the northeast corner of the immense Luis Maria Baca Grant No. 4. Several nineteenth-century surveyors attempted to locate the corner but chose instead to label the vicinity "Unsurveyable" and "Unaccessible Mountains."

The Luis Maria Baca Grant No. 4 was one of four grants of 100,000 acres each made to Don Luis Maria de Vaca by the

Mount Adams may appear deceptively low heading north up the drainage north of Willow Creek Lake.

From the saddle between it and its western subpeak, Mount Adams' prominent summit cap beckons.

government of Mexico to encourage northern settlement after Mexico declared its independence from Spain. Like many of the Spanish land grants, its story was characterized by ownership disputes and competing uses. Mount Adams is named after George H. Adams, a long-time manager of the grant in the late 1800s.

The town of Crestone began just north of the grant boundary in 1879 and survived the ups and downs of at least three separate gold and silver rushes to the region. Crestone, which at one time even boasted a Denver and Rio Grande spur, is the sole survivor of a number of towns which sprang up as products of rushes both on and off the Baca grant. One town, Liberty, located just east of the grant boundary, was founded by disgruntled miners from Duncan, who were evicted from the grant by owners more interested in raising Herefords than in mining ore.

While extensive mining was done near Mount Adams, the first recorded ascent occurred in July of 1916 when Albert

"Yes, I know, Tim, Gary is always eating." Summit of Mount Adams looking northeast.

Ellingwood and company arrived in the Willow Creek drainage south of the peak to tackle the unclimbed slopes of Kit Carson Peak and the Crestones. Ellingwood's account of the whole adventure makes interesting reading in the June 1925 issue of *Trail and Timberline*. After an ascent of Kit Carson, and while preparing to take on the Crestones, Ellingwood and several others climbed the eastern point of what he described as the "two symmetrical sentinels" north of the upper Willow Creek Basin. The description fits Mount Adams and its 13,544-foot western subpeak. From its summit Ellingwood found "a fine panorama of the Kit Carson peaks." Indeed, you cannot hike beneath the rugged walls of the Willow Creek Basin without a longing to have been with Ellingwood here in 1916, when, in his words, he arrived "fed in part by tales of peaks unclimbed and peaks unclimbable."

THE ROUTES
Rio Grande National Forest
Crestone Peak 7½ Quad
Horn Peak 7½ Quad

120

Willow Creek: From just south of Moffat on Colorado 17, drive east for twelve miles to the town of Crestone. (Follow the signs for Baca Grande.) Upon entering town, the main road jogs north (left), east (right), and north (left) again before coming to a stop sign at the main town intersection. The post office is on the northeast corner of this intersection. After turning right at the post office intersection, drive east for one mile on a road which rapidly becomes a dirt washboard. Although the road is passable in a four-wheel drive for another one mile to the trailhead, it is extremely rocky and rough, and you may find it just as fast to park and walk the remaining mile.

From the trailhead, essentially two miles from the post office, the Willow Creek Trail crosses south over Crestone Creek and then climbs east into the Willow Creek drainage. Near the east end of Willow Creek Park, the trail splits again with the south (right-hand) fork descending into the park and

Crestone Peak (left) beyond the Willow Creek Basin and Kit Carson Peak to the right, from summit of Mount Adams.

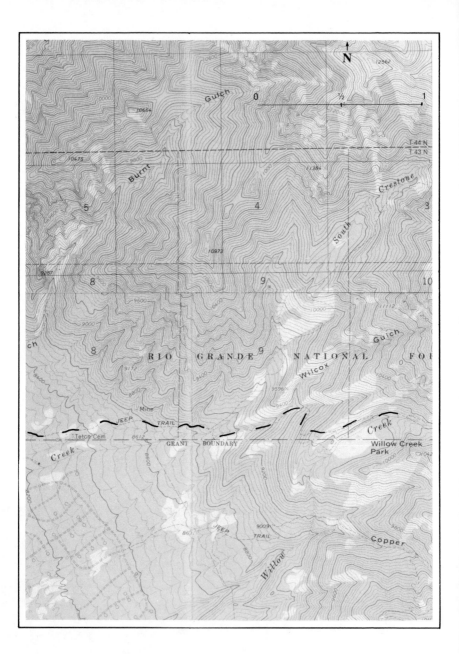

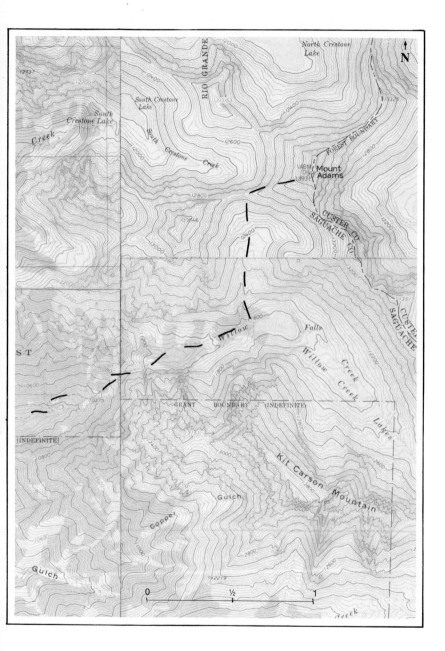

following the Willow Creek drainage east to Willow Creek Lake. The left-hand trail stays high above the wetness of the drainage and switchbacks its way to the lake. The latter is certainly the drier route if you do not mind the switchbacks. Both routes will take you to lower Willow Creek Lake at 11,564 feet, four miles from the trailhead.

From just east of the outlet of the lake, climb directly north up what is first a grassy slope into a high basin. The saddle between Mount Adams to the east and Peak 13,546 to the west is directly north. From here, Mount Adams looks deceptively low; however, continue directly north to the saddle and do not be drawn northeast by the basin drainage, confusing Mount Adams for Peak 13,546. From the saddle, Mount Adams is one-half mile and a 1,000-foot gain in elevation to the east. Stay primarily on the ridge, skirting the final cut and summit block on the south (right) and reaching the summit from the south. There are fine views of Kit Carson and the Crestones from the summit.

Trailhead, and end of four-wheel drive, to summit: 5½ miles
Elevation gain: 5,100 feet
(Route description from August climb)

The saddle west of Mount Adams may also be reached via the South Crestone Creek Trail, which runs northeast from the Willow Creek trailhead described above.

Part 3
The Western Slope

The Western Slope is unique. It is, in the words of historians Duane Vandenbusche and Duane Smith, "a land alone"—alone in the unprecedented spectacle of its diverse beauty and alone in its lack of independent political and economic power, which has left it a frequent pawn of outside interests. Most certainly, among its vast canyonlands and snowy summits is some of the grandest wilderness left in America.

At the heart of the Western Slope are the Elk Mountains. From challenging Cathedral Peak in the east to colorful Mount Owen in the west, the Elk Mountains and their deserving southwest spur, the West Elk Range, are red, rugged, and rotten. Backpacking and climbing opportunities abound, with Hagerman Peak, Thunder Pyramid, and Hayden Peak spectacular alternatives to the Fourteeners of the range.

To the south, the San Juan Mountains dominate southwestern Colorado like a giant fist of gnarled knuckles punching up through the earth's crust. From Rio Grande Pyramid, the ranges of the San Juan unfold to form a jagged circle now just as they did for the Wheeler and Hayden parties in 1874. Family climbs such as Engineer Mountain near Cold Bank Pass and Hesperus Mountain in the La Plata Range have been expertly chronicled by Paul Pixler in *Hiking Trails of Southwestern Colorado*. As for the rigorous ascents—peaks with names like Arrow, Vestal, Storm King, and Silex—they cannot be done justice in these pages and thus are left for "the next time."

CATHEDRAL PEAK
13,943 Feet
Elk Range

For want of fifty-seven feet, Cathedral Peak does not qualify for inclusion on the list of Elk Range Fourteeners, but its character equals that of its higher neighbors. Cathedral Peak's jagged north ridge and its crumbling northeast face make red, rugged, and rotten an apt description indeed. Snow stays in the couloirs until late in the year, and ice axes and crampons may be necessary to reach the south ridge in all but August or September.

Cathedral Peak lives up to its name on this approach from the southeast. The route crosses the talus in the foreground and circles left into the basin behind the impressive towers.

Tim Duffy ascends the prominent couloir en route to the summit of Cathedral Peak. Note the snow remaining in the upper reaches of the couloir on this mid-August 1983 climb. *Gary R. Koontz photo.*

Henry Gannett, a member of the Hayden Survey, led a party up nearby Castle Peak in 1873, but apparently they did not attempt Cathedral Peak. Gannett's party did name its neighbor to the north after their leader, Ferdinand V. Hayden, one of several peaks named for him throughout the west.

Mining was once intense in this area of the Elk Range. The Castle Creek drainage to the east of Cathedral Peak was a part of the Pearl Pass route to the Gunnison country. Electric Pass, which crosses the saddle between Cathedral and Hayden peaks, was a miner's trail connecting the Castle Creek and Conundrum drainages. In 1880, miners laid out the town of Castle Forks City just east of the peak, but as the boom of the early eighties crested, the town changed its name to Ashcroft. Two major silver mines, the Montezuma and the Tam O'Shanter, both properties of H.A.W. Tabor, insured the town's success for a time, but, when the Denver and Rio Grande Railroad finally reached Aspen in 1887, Ashcroft's

127

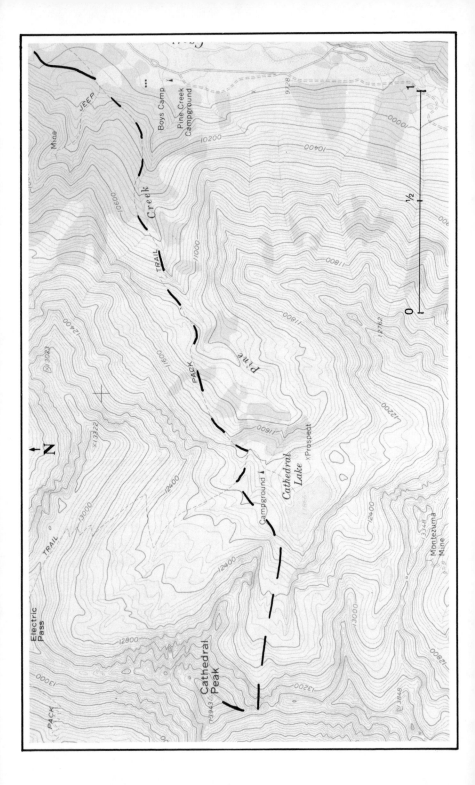

future and the importance of the Pearl Pass road faded. The Aspen Historical Society deserves high praise for its continuing efforts to preserve what remains of Ashcroft.

THE ROUTES
White River National Forest
Hayden Peak 7½ Quad

Cathedral Lake/Southeast Couloir: From just west of Aspen on Colorado 82, at the junction of 82 and the Maroon Creek and Castle Creek roads, drive south up the paved Castle Creek road 11 miles to the ghost town of Ashcroft. Continue. one mile beyond Ashcroft and turn west (right) up a dirt road which switchbacks three-quarters of a mile to the parking area at the Cathedral Lake trailhead. (This new road has been added on the map.)

From the trailhead, hike west on the Cathedral Lake Trail two miles to the junction of the Cathedral Lake and Electric Pass trails. From here, the object is to reach a faint trail which climbs atop the moraine almost due west and leads into the basin southeast of Cathedral Peak. The trail can be reached either by following the Electric Pass Trail for almost one-quarter of a mile and then dropping west across a drainage and onto the moraine, or by continuing to Cathedral Lake, recrossing Pine Creek near the lake's outlet, and then mounting the moraine.

The moraine trail and main drainage leads west over generally stable talus beneath some spectacular walls and towers. At the head of this basin, a prominent couloir leads to Cathedral's summit ridge just to the north of two large blocktowers. *This couloir requires extreme caution!* In the early season an ice axe is mandatory, and rope and/or crampons may be desirable. Later in the season, the couloir turns into loose scree, melting ice, and typical Elk Range rotten. Approximately one-half the way up the couloir, a right-hand branch offers an alternative route to reach the summit ridge. While the rock in this right-hand branch is somewhat more secure than in the main couloir, the route is steeper. The better passage is probably to continue up the main couloir to the ridge.

Once atop the ridge, climb north one-quarter of a mile to the summit. The ridge is crumbly, but presents no major problems with several points being easily skirted.

From the summit there is a fine view of Pyramid Peak and the Maroon Bells, both to the west; of Castle Peak to the south; and of the entire Sawatch Range to the east. Continue to exercise the appropriate cautions on the descent down the couloir. This climb is only for experienced parties.

Trailhead to summit: 4 miles
Elevation gain: 4,100 feet
(Route description from August climb)

While the ridge north from Cathedral to Electric Pass looks terribly broken and jagged, it appears that most obstacles can be skirted on the west. This may offer an interesting alternate route.

TEOCALLI MOUNTAIN
13,208 Feet
Elk Mountains

Teocalli Mountain rises along the southern edge of the Elk Mountains. From its summit, an unparalleled view of the Elk Range Fourteeners unfolds to the north.

The mountain was climbed and named during the summer of 1873 by a Hayden Survey party which included William Byers of the *Rocky Mountain News*. They chose the name "Teocalli" for the mountain's resemblance to the flat-topped pyramids which the Aztecs of Mexico used in their religious rituals. The Hayden team showed similar originality in naming Italian

The grassy slopes of Teocalli Mountain looking north from West Brush Creek. *Gary R. Koontz photo.*

Mountain to the east—its horizontal stripes of red rock, white snow, and green vegetation reminded them of the Italian flag.

Less than a decade after this visit by the Hayden Survey, the mining boom hit the Gunnison country. Miners swarmed into the area just south of Teocalli Mountain. Valiant efforts were soon underway to construct a wagon road across Pearl Pass on the mountain's east flank to link Crested Butte with Aspen. The road ran up Middle Brush Creek between Teocalli and Italian mountains, across Pearl Pass, and down the Castle Creek drainage to Ashcroft and Aspen. The narrow, winding road—in places little more than a thin shelf cut out of the

131

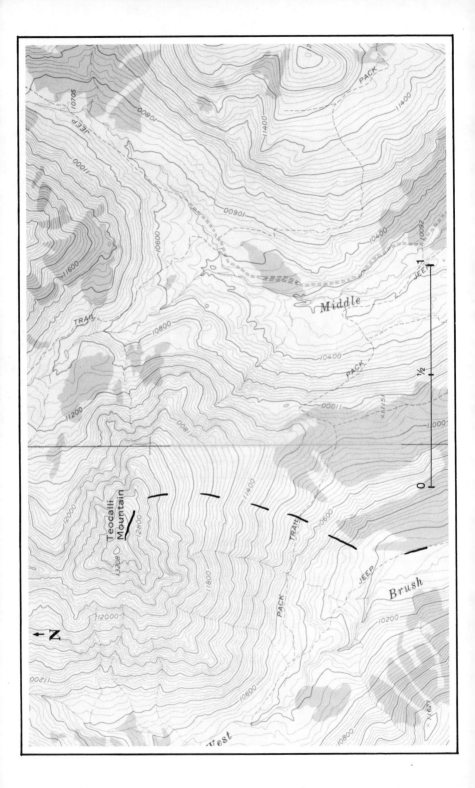

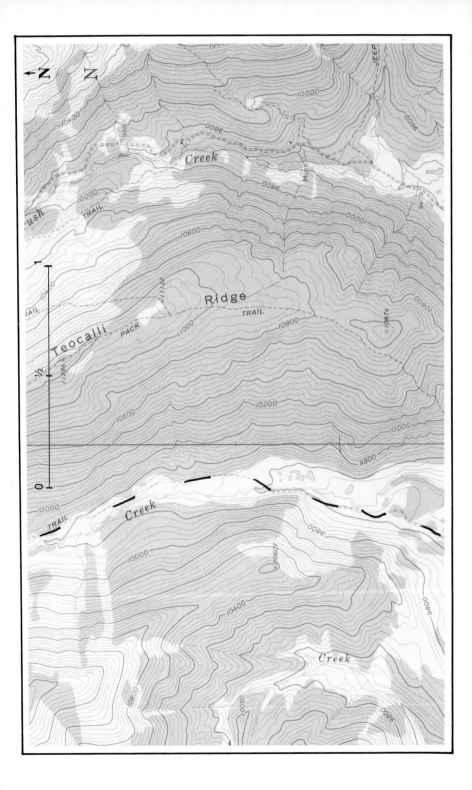

mountainside—was a freighter's nightmare. Although some wagons negotiated the pass in the early 1880s, after that, the route quickly deteriorated into a jack trail.

THE ROUTES—with Gary Koontz
Gunnison National Forest
Gothic 7½ Quad
Pearl Pass 7½ Quad

West Brush Creek: Teocalli Mountain is a moderate climb offering fine views of the Elk Range. Drive north from Gunnison twenty-six miles on Colorado 135 or go south from Crested Butte two miles on the same road. At the Crested Butte airport turnoff, go east up the drainage of the East River on the East River road. It passes Mount Crested Butte on the south and soon becomes a forest access road. There is considerable construction in the first few miles; so be wary.

Although not a hard-core jeep route, the East River road becomes rutted and rough in spots. After 4.3 miles it comes to a junction near the Brush Creek Cow Camp. Take the right-hand (east) fork, which ascends the Brush Creek drainage. After almost one mile, this road divides again with the right (east) branch ascending Middle Brush Creek bound for Pearl Pass and the left (west) branch ascending West Brush Creek into the basin west of Teocalli Mountain. Either route will give you access to the peak, but the West Brush Creek drainage is probably more direct. Take this north for two miles, then park where the road crosses the creek and deteriorates.

Cross the creek and follow the old road at least one and one-half miles before choosing a route north up the grassy slopes. Head for the shoulder east of the cliffs and then follow the ridge crest west to the summit.

The summit view is a dandy. All the Fourteeners in the Elk Range are visible with Castle Peak just a drainage away. The development near the Crested Butte Ski Area is visible to the southwest.

Creek crossing to summit: 3 miles
Elevation gain: 3,600 feet
(Route description from June climb)

MOUNT OWEN
13,058 Feet
Ruby Range—Elk Mountains

Mount Owen is the high point of an eight-mile chain of ruby-colored mountains which run south from the main concentration of the Elk Range into the Gunnison country. In the spring of 1879, the peaceful valley below Mount Owen came suddenly alive with prospectors. For the most part, they were men down on their luck, most having failed to strike it rich in the Leadville boom. By the end of the summer, Dick Irwin, a man always in the advance guard of mining booms, had given his name to a townsite on the south shore of an emerald lake. By the following spring, the rush to Irwin was on and the "Big Four" mines of the Ruby district had begun trying to outdo one another with boasts of rich ruby silver ore.

The mines and their discoverers were a colorful lot. Jim Brennand and Charlie Deffenbaugh located the Ruby Chief first a half-mile northwest of the lake. A.T. Gilkerson paused by the creek north of the lake and stumbled onto the rich ledge of ore which became the Lead Chief. West of the lake, beneath the slopes of Ruby Peak, the Bullion King operated with less boasts and more production. From 1879 to 1891, when it was destroyed by an avalanche, it was the only mine of the "Big Four" to return a profit. Finally, there was the Forest Queen, the reigning sovereign of the Ruby-Irwin district, located southeast of the townsite.

Irwin quickly attracted John E. Phillips, one of the great newspaper editors of the region. Phillips founded the *Elk Mountain Pilot* and boldly declared to the town's special interests: "We do not belong to our patrons, the Pilot is wholly

Mount Owen (center) with Ruby Peak (left) and Purple Peak (right) rise above the waters of Lake Irwin.

our own; those who like it can take it, those who don't can let it alone."

Phillips was well known for his wit, as evidenced by the report of an encounter with a woman skier on the slopes of Mount Owen. Clothed in dress and petticoats, the woman took a bad spill, showing off some shapely legs and dainty undergarments in the process. Phillips laughed boisterously, which caused the woman to retort, "Sir, I have seen enough of you to know that you are no gentleman!" The witty Phillips replied, "Madam, I too have seen enough of you to know that you are no gentleman!"

The boom which brought Phillips to Irwin was short-lived. Alas, for Dick Irwin, Jim Brennand, and others, the Ruby

Chief, Lead Chief, Bullion King, and Forest Queen were not the El Dorados of boast and dream. By 1882, the boom had gone to bust and Irwin went quietly about becoming a ghost town.

Mining activity, however, has continued to the present day. Four claims—the Teller, Taylor, May Bird, and Grace—were worked high above Green Lake in the basin between Mount Owen and Ruby Peak. On the west side of Mount Owen, the General Sayles Mine and Little Gracie were located in Silver Basin and were reached from Irwin by a crumbling pass known as St. Gabriel's Gate, just north of Purple Peak.

Today, the valley beneath Mount Owen is a microcosm of competing values and life-styles. You can stand among the rotting timbers of mine portals and view a new, barn-like ski lodge. Or you can watch a determined John H. Hahn, the "Grand Old Man of the Forest Queen," still go about operating the venerable mine. If you look east beyond the Forest Queen boundary, you can see Mount Emmons, the site of a controversial molybdenum deposit controlled by AMAX, one of the world's largest mining companies. What a contrast! John Hahn, one of the very few individual prospectors still on the trail of El Dorado, and AMAX, the corporate giant with techniques Dick Irwin would never have understood.

THE ROUTES
Gunnison National Forest
Oh-Be-Joyful 7½ Quad
Marcellina Mountain 7½ Quad

Lake Irwin: From the Forest Service campground at Lake Irwin, seven miles west of Crested Butte, hike north along an old road which makes a turn left (west) at the ruins of the Ruby Chief Mine and then runs north along the eastern slopes of Ruby Peak, Mount Owen, and Purple Peak. In early spring, avoid the broad avalanche chute coming off Ruby Peak. To include Ruby Peak in the climb, hike northwest up the rounded southeast ridge, left (south) of the prominent cliffs. Once above

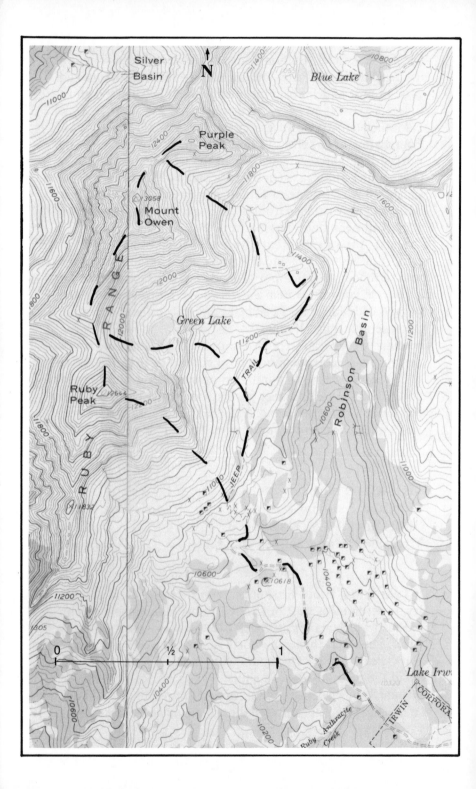

the cliffs, follow the ridge west a quarter of a mile to the summit. Climbing Ruby Peak adds 500 feet of elevation to the Mount Owen climb.

For Mount Owen alone, continue up the road past the northeast cliffs of Ruby Peak and then contour west into the basin of Green Lake. Circle the lake and climb west toward the Ruby-Owen saddle at 12,200 feet. The route becomes increasingly steep and loose the further north you hit the Owen ridge. From the saddle, climb north along the summit ridge to the top. From the summit, the half-dome mound of Marcellina Mountain and the canyon of Ruby-Anthracite Creek are impressive views to the west.

Descend the same way, or, if you wish to scale another peak, scramble north off the summit and follow a crumbling ridge a third of a mile to Purple Peak, 12,800 feet (not to be confused with Purple Mountain, 12,985 feet at the northern end of the Ruby Range.) There is a rather impressive view of Mount Owen from Purple Peak. A tricky descent is possible down a loose and crumbling couloir—typical Elk Range rotten—from the Owen-Purple saddle. The drainage from this couloir leads back to the road paralleling the peaks. The Ruby Range is prime avalanche country, and early season climbs require caution and ice axes.

Lake Irwin to Mount Owen summit via Ruby Peak:
3 miles
Elevation gain: 3,200 feet
(Route description from October climb)

WEST ELK PEAK
13,035 Feet
West Elk Mountains

West Elk Peak is the high point in the West Elk Mountains which run north and south through the West Elk Primitive Area northwest of Gunnison. To the north are the deserving

Looking west to the summit of West Elk Peak along the grassy ridge from the 12,968-foot sub-peak. *Gary R. Koontz photo.*

twin summits of the Beckwith Peaks and the unusual Castles. To the south, the West Elks roll over a prolific succession of Baldies—North Baldy, Middle Baldy, Middle Baldy Mountain, and South Baldy. The approach to the peak via Mill Creek is a delightful assembly of cascading waterfalls, leafy aspens, and towering crowns and spires.

West Elk Peak was first climbed by Indians or miners. North of the peak, the Utes had a favorite trail which crossed from the North Fork of the Gunnison River via Kebler Pass to the Ohio Creek drainage of the main Gunnison. Miners scoured the country northeast of the peak during the silver boom of the early 1880s. The spring of 1880 found the Ohio Pass road at the mouth of Mill Creek jammed with a rush of prospectors bound for the boom town of Irwin. Silver's promise soon waned, but

From near Storm Pass the Castles rise dramatically above the Mill Creek Valley. In the background is the Anthracite Range west of Ohio Pass and beyond it the Elk Range. *Gary R. Koontz photo.*

coal near Floresta enticed the Denver and Rio Grande Railway to build to Crested Butte shortly after it arrived in Gunnison in August of 1881. Later, the Denver South Park and Pacific built up Ohio Creek to the coal mines of Baldwin, the farthest west the railroad ever progressed. Today, the West Elk Mountains still harbor untold mineral wealth which may produce a battle over their wilderness designation.

THE ROUTES—with Gary Koontz
Gunnison National Forest
Squirrel Creek 7½ Quad
West Elk Peak 7½ Quad

141

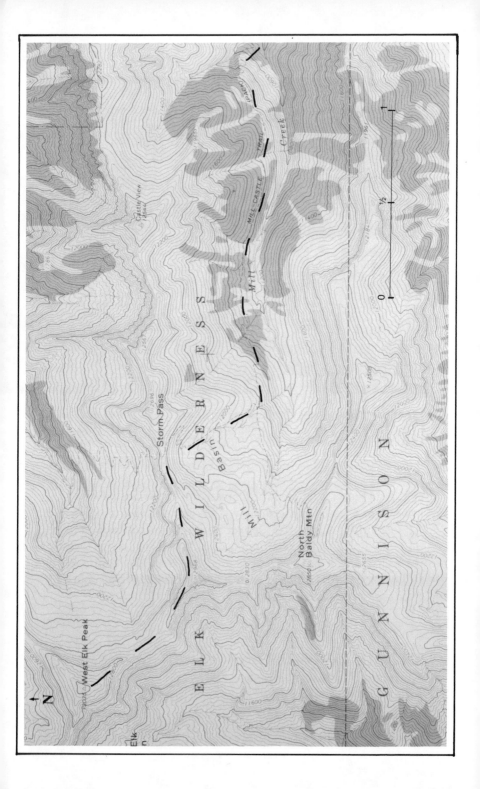

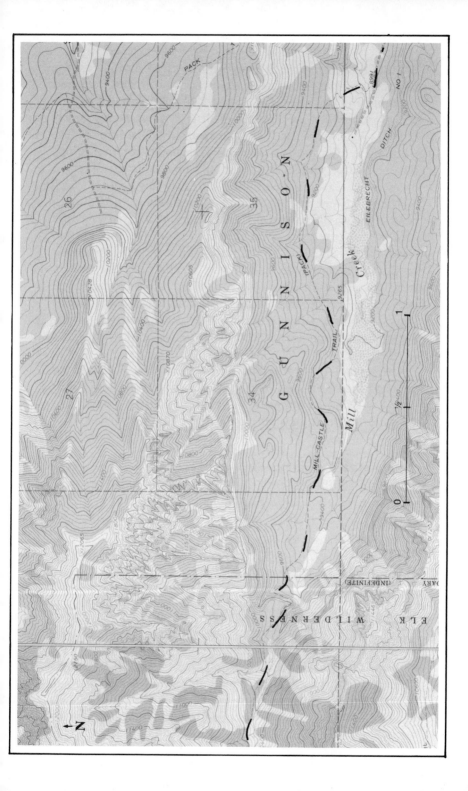

Mill Creek: Drive north from Gunnison on Colorado 135 for two miles to the Ohio Creek road. Turn northwest (left) and continue up Ohio Creek for 8.8 miles, turning west (left) up the well-signed Mill Creek road, which is a forest access across much private property. If the gates are closed, be sure to close them again after passing through. The road is rough in spots, but with care, passenger cars should be able to go the three miles to the parking area by the Forest Service gate.

The Mill Creek Trail to Storm Pass begins here and follows a road along an old irrigation ditch. After one mile, in a pasture area where cow trails can cause confusion, the trail crosses north over Mill Creek. Look for the trail scar on the northwest bank. Once across the creek, you should find the trail in excellent condition and can easily follow it to a campsite area near mile 7. Here, the Storm Pass Trail turns north (right) while the North Baldy Mountain Trail continues west. There are many camping areas as the Storm Pass Trail switchbacks north to the pass.

Upon reaching Storm Pass, the view west will dictate the route to the summit of West Elk Peak. Follow the ridge west over a 12,968-foot subpeak and continue on the grassy ridge 1.6 miles to the high point of the West Elk Mountains.

Trailhead to summit: 9 miles
Elevation gain: 4,400 feet
(Route description from September climb)

7-7-2001
RIO GRANDE PYRAMID
13,821 Feet
San Juan Range

With the exception of Uncompahgre Peak, Rio Grande Pyramid is unrivalled as the outstanding landmark of the San Juans. Its central location in the heart of the range and its relative isolation above the upper Rio Grande Valley provide an unobstructed, 360-degree panorama of Colorado's last great mountain refuge. Beginning with Redcloud and Sunshine peaks, almost due north from the summit, and moving westward, the horizon is studded by Uncompahgre, Wetterhorn, Sneffels, the Wilsons, the Grenadiers, and the Needles. To the northeast, Bristol Head is lower but impressive, while to the southeast, the Continental Divide drifts off in the distance toward New Mexico.

For a long time, Rio Grande Pyramid was a landmark for the Utes, who traveled a well-worn trail across Weminuche Pass between the headwaters of the Los Pinos River and the

Rio Grande Pyramid, one of the dominant landmarks of the San Juans, looking west. One circles the drainage to the left, mounts the hump below the peak, and climbs almost directly west up its east face.

Rio Grande. Historian Marshall Sprague speculates that mountain man James Ohio Pattie may have made the first documented crossing of the pass in 1827. Unfortunately, Pattie's account of the crossing, while en route from southwestern Colorado to Santa Fe, is also replete with tales of the Yellowstone and points north, leaving some doubt as to his exact location, if not his consumption of Taos Lightning.

In the summer of 1874, men who did know where they were descended on Rio Grande Pyramid in force. Lieutenant William Marshall's division of the Wheeler Survey came first and made the earliest recorded ascent of the peak. Marshall wrote that it was "one of the handsomest and most symmetrical cones in Colorado."

Later that summer, on August 22, Franklin Rhoda led a crew from the Hayden Survey to the summit. There he found the Wheeler Survey cairn and correctly surmised that "the fact that the monument was on the true summit indicated the fact that its builder was something else than a common miner." Rhoda, like Marshall, was impressed by the mountain's shape. "Its pyramidal form is almost perfect, while at the same time there is just enough bluff intermingled with the debris slopes to give relief without the usual accompaniment of coarseness."

The Wheeler Survey, in its typical fashion of seeking to honor men, named the mountain "Simpson's Pyramid." It was the more appropriate Hayden name, however, which stuck, and Simpson had to be content with a smaller summit north of the pyramid. The Hayden men finished their season in the San Juans by traveling from the Durango area to Denver across the broad flats of Weminuche Pass in the midst of an October snowstorm.

Today, aside from the passage of backpackers and hikers, the principal activity atop Weminuche Pass is the quiet flow of the Raber Lohr ditch, which carries Western Slope water from the Los Pinos River eastward across the Continental Divide into Weminuche Creek.

THE ROUTES
Rio Grande National Forest
Rio Grande Pyramid 7½ Quad
Weminuche Pass 7½ Quad

Weminuche Pass: From a place twenty-four miles south of Lake City or nineteen miles west of Creede on Colorado 149, drive west on Forest Service 520 eleven miles to Thirty Mile Campground. Camping is also available two miles east of Thirty Mile at River Bend Campground or seven miles west at Lost Trail Campground.

From the trailhead at Thirty Mile Campground, climb west along Rio Grande Reservoir one and one-half miles to the mouth of Weminuche Creek, then go south up the creek to the summit of the pass, a total of five miles. (The sign atop the pass insists that the distance is six miles.) The first two miles are moderately steep, but a scattering of columbines and Indian paintbrush should ease the burden of a heavy pack. The remaining distance to the pass is gentle.

Continue south across the pass for nine-tenths of a mile until the trail splits, the east (left) branch immediately crossing the Raber Lohr ditch and the west (right) branch heading up Rincon de la Vaca. (There is a trail junction prior to this where the east fork does not cross the ditch and the west deadends at an old cabin.) About seven-tenths of a mile up Rincon de la Vaca, the trail emerges from the trees to provide a stunning view of the pyramid and, to the south, a unique formation called "the window," a huge, symmetrical cut in the ridge running south from the pyramid. To the north is a prominent subpeak known as "Fools Pyramid."

Continue on the trail for two miles until it climbs above timberline, crosses the main creek, and curves abruptly south to cross the pyramid's east ridge. From here the route-finding is a matter of choice. The most obvious option is to mount the hump of the pyramid's east flank and then scamper up the northeast ridge another mile to the top. The summit ridge is steep and broken, but of generally stable volcanic rock. As promised, the view from the summit is spectacular.

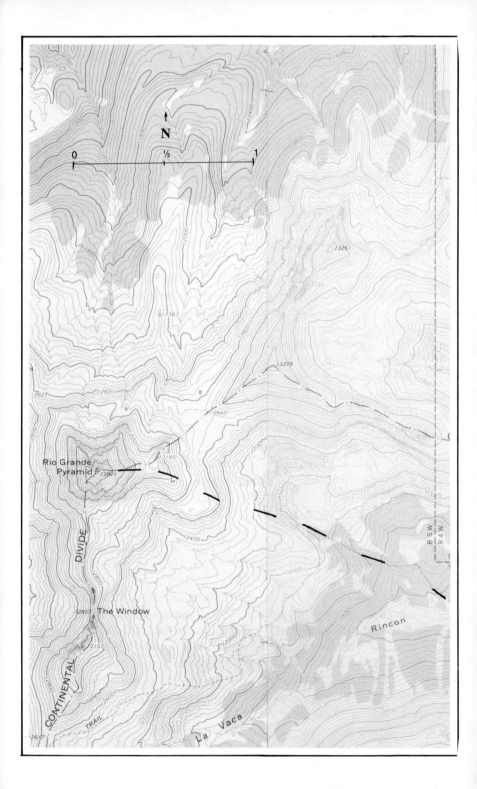

N

0 ½ 1

13261

13130

13278

12627 2600 12645

13185
Rio Grande
Pyramid 13801

DIVIDE

12857 The Window

13157

CONTINENTAL

TRAIL

12671

La Vaca

Rincon

R 5 W
R 4 W

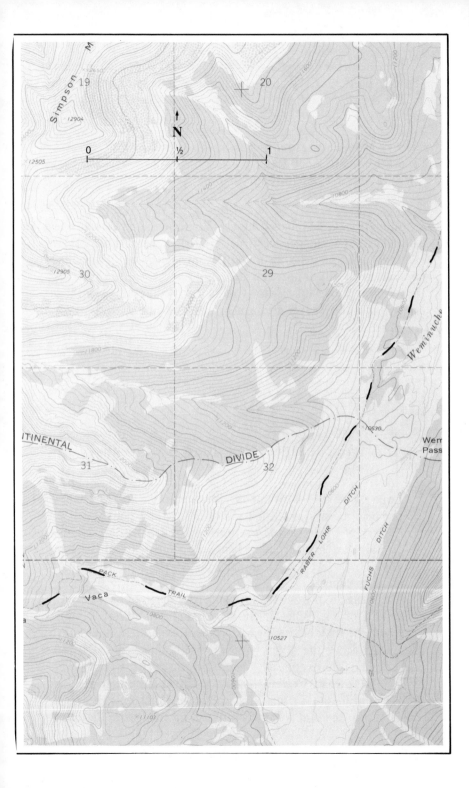

I recommend a one-day climb of the peak for only the *most* hardy, particularly when a number of fine campsites exist along Weminuche Pass.

Thirty Mile Campground to summit: 10 miles
Elevation gain: 4,500 feet
(Route description from July climb)

While I have climbed only the Weminuche approach, the Ute Creek drainage with its trailhead near Lost Trail Campground seems to be a viable approach as well. The chief problems of this approach are finding the route onto the mountain from East Ute Creek and contending with a generally more rugged character of the mountain's upper reaches.

LONE CONE
12,613 Feet
San Miguel Range—San Juan Mountains

Lone Cone rises with uncharacteristic grace and symmetry above arid mesa tops at the head of Disappointment Creek. It is the dot of the exclamation mark made by the San Miguel Mountains as they thrust eastward into the heart of the San Juans. To the west are the canyons of Utah and the great Colorado Plateau.

The location of Lone Cone prompted Lieutenant William L. Marshall of the Wheeler Survey to name it "West Point," although he may have been also remembering his alma mater. Marshall was quite taken with the mountain's symmetry and described its sharp cone as "the most beautiful peak I have ever seen." Renowned western historian David Lavender echoed those sentiments in his first book, *One Man's West*, a fascinating account of growing up in the range country

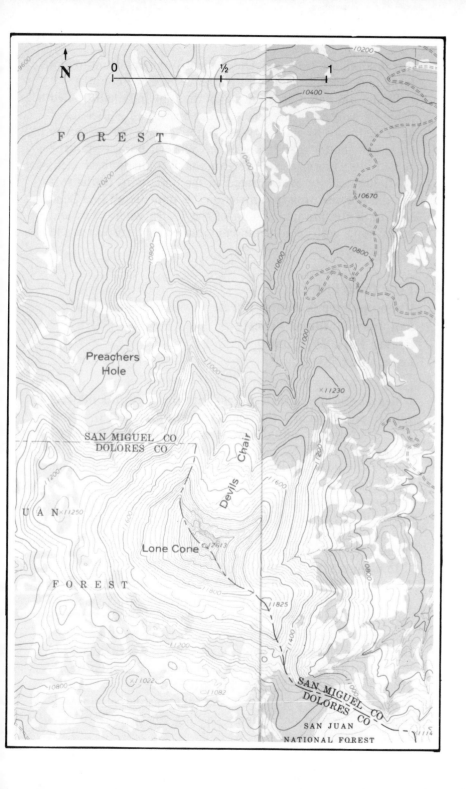

N

0   ½   1

F O R E S T

9600

10200

10400

10200

10600

10670

10800

Preachers
Hole

11000

11000

×11230

SAN MIGUEL CO
DOLORES CO

Devils Chair

11600

11200

U A N ×11250

1600

Lone Cone ⋌12613

11800

F O R E S T

11800 ⌁11825

11200

10800

×11022 ⌁11082

11400

10800

SAN MIGUEL CO
DOLORES CO

SAN JUAN
NATIONAL FOREST

⌁11114

surrounding the peak. Lavender spent summers rounding up cattle and driving them through the Lone Cone country.

The mountain's first ascent was perhaps by Indians attracted either by its prominence as a lookout or by the significance of its isolation. The name "West Point" was a noble try by Marshall—better than many of the Wheeler names—but the name Lone Cone was so entirely apt that it could not be denied.

Mining activity concentrated in the San Juans to the east and did not make a large impact on the immediate Lone Cone area until the uranium boom of the 1950s, when jeeps and crazed souls with geiger counters replaced the prospector and his burro.

THE ROUTES
Uncompahgre National Forest
San Juan National Forest
Beaver Park 7½ Quad
Lone Cone 7½ Quad

Beaver Park/Spectacle Creek: Pity the poor mountaineer who one day decides that there are no peaks left to climb! Indeed, everyone should always have a list of "I've always wanted to go there" summits. Lone Cone has been on my list since it was a welcome landmark on my first cross-country solo flight some dozen years ago. While I have not climbed it as of this writing, I desperately wanted to include it in this collection. Thus, it becomes both the end and the beginning—the concluding peak of this presentation and the first on the list for the next climbing season.

In planning the trip, I will consider that the mountain should make a good snow climb early in the season. Two routes present themselves. The first is described by Bob Ormes and involves climbing either the north or northeast ridge from the Beaver Park road. The other approaches the mountain from the west up Spectacle Creek via a trail which switchbacks to timberline at the base of the west shoulder. Private property access may be a concern on this latter route.

If I don't see you on Lone Cone next season, perhaps we'll meet on "the next one." Here's wishing you many!

Index